Millennial Marriages

"A Military Relationship"

JARRON WEBSTER, M.B.A.

THE TAMPA
BOW TIE GUY

Published by Richter Publishing LLC
www.richterpublishing.com

Book Cover Design: Richter Publishing

Editors: Monica San Nicolas, Natalie Meyer & Margarita Martinez

ISBN: 1945812435

ISBN-13: 9781945812439

DISCLAIMER

This book is designed to provide information on marriages/ relationships only. This information is provided and sold with the knowledge that the publisher and author do not offer any legal or medical advice. In the case of a need for any such expertise consult with the appropriate professional. This book does not contain all information available on the subject. This book has not been created to be specific to any individual people or organization's situation or needs. Reasonable efforts have been made to make this book as accurate as possible. However, there may be typographical and or content errors. Therefore, this book should serve only as a general guide. This book contains information that might be dated or erroneous and is intended only to educate and entertain. The author and publisher shall have no liability or responsibility to any person or entity regarding any loss or damage incurred, or alleged to have incurred, directly or indirectly, by the information contained in this book or as a result of anyone acting or failing to act upon the information in this book. You hereby agree never to sue and to hold the author and publisher harmless from any and all claims arising out of the information contained in this book. You hereby agree to be bound by this disclaimer, covenant not to sue and release. You may return this book within the guaranteed time period for a full refund. In the interest of full disclosure, this book contains affiliate links that might pay the author or publisher a commission upon any purchase from the company. While the author and publisher take no responsibility for any virus or technical issues that could be caused by such links, the business practices of these companies and/or the performance of any product or service, the author or publisher have used the product or service and make a recommendation in good faith based on that experience. All characters appearing in this work have given permission. Any resemblance to other real persons, living or dead, is purely coincidental. The opinions and stories in this book are the views of the author and not those of the publisher.

DEDICATION

I'd like to dedicate this book to my family and friends, who gave me any type of support when I needed it. This is dedicated to the mother of my children, who is a very special woman. My two sons are the reason I wake up every day and they are the reason I was able to complete this book!

This is dedicated to anybody who ever believed in me and also to those who doubted me. I dedicate this to having faith in yourself. If you can believe it, you can conceive it.

CONTENTS

ACKNOWLEDGEMENTS

I would like to thank a few of my closest friends and family who helped me stay motivated throughout this process. I would like to thank Richter Publishing for helping me make this dream a reality. There's a long list of people I would like to thank, but most of all, I have to give thanks to God and the universe for this "Million Dollar Idea."

INTRODUCTION

Over the years, marriage has been viewed in many different lights. It now seems that marriage is something people do for multiple reasons, and coming together in harmony is harder and harder. It can be even more difficult for people serving in the military. The reality of being apart can pressure people into getting married sooner than they normally would in order to stay together.

When young people realize they are about to leave and be without the person they love, they start thinking irrationally, regardless of what advice they may be receiving from outside sources. Family, friends, and even some mentors have trouble getting through to a Millennial when they have what they consider "a plan." Talking a Millennial out of a marriage is quite the challenge because, for the most part, when a Millennial has their mind made up, that's pretty much the end of it.

In this book I am going to share with you a story about two people deeply in love, Mark and Wendy. Mark is leaving soon to his permanent duty station in the military. Neither Mark nor Wendy want to leave each other, and they've already been separated by basic and technical training. What decisions will be made by the couple when facing this military stigma?

1

LET'S GET MARRIED

"We ain't getting no younger, we might as well do it ..."
-Jagged Edge
"Let's Get Married"

As the sun rises, rays of light beam through the blinds onto Wendy Smith's face. When she opens her eyes, she immediately regrets forgetting to grab those new curtains the day before. She turns to face the other way and as soon as she settles back into the pillow, her iPhone alarm rings so loudly, she just knows her family hears it.

"All right, already!" Face buried in her pillow, she reaches for her phone and accidentally knocks it off the nightstand. "Of course," she says. Slowly raising her head, she peeks at the floor and grabs her phone, quickly hitting *stop* on her alarm. She sees a text notification from Mark saying, **"I can't wait to see you."**

Feeling like she's received a burst of energy from the message, Wendy flips over and texts back, **"I love you! Now hurry up!"**

After the message sends, Wendy checks her Facebook notifications. She sees that her mom commented on one of her posts and she shakes her head, saying, "Why does everybody have access to social media?" She scrolls down her newsfeed for a few minutes before she switches over to look at her Instagram.

"Wendy! Are you up?" yells her mother.

"Yes, Mom, I'm up," Wendy calls back. "I'll be down in a minute."

Mrs. Smith replies, "You better pick up the pace if you're going to make class on time!"

Wendy finally realizes what day it is and slips out of the bed, her warm feet touching the cold laminate flooring. She quickly slides her feet into her soft pink bunny slippers, wiggles her toes, and then she's off to the races. While brushing her teeth, she squints her eyes a little, trying to remember if she completed all of her homework last night ...

She smiles, remembering the long conversation she and Mark

had, then shrugs her shoulders at the homework attempt. She's finding it hard to concentrate on what needs to be done for school when all she can do is think about Mark and what he's been experiencing. She just wants him to hurry back to her so they can be together again.

Picking up a little momentum, Wendy picks out her outfit for the day a little faster than usual: a dazzling yellow sundress with white heels and a white flower hairpin to top everything off.

"That's what I'm wearing later," she says to herself. "Now let's get into these scrubs and get to business." Wendy is very excited about pursuing her dream to become a nurse. She's finally at the tail end of her schooling and is looking forward to working more hands-on during her final stages of clinicals.

"Wendyyyyyy ... let's goooo!" her mother screams up the stairs. "I'll leave you, and I'm not kidding!"

Wendy chuckles because her mom makes the same statement regularly, but never follows through. As she walks down the stairs, sliding her hand down the smooth wooden railing, she says, "You can stop yelling now, Mother; we wouldn't want your blood pressure to get too high."

Mrs. Smith responds, "Don't 'Mother' me, all right? I have to try to get you to class on time while trying to get myself to work on time also."

"Mom, you don't go to work until noon, and you only

work for four hours at that consignment shop you call a job."

"It gets me away from your father for a few hours, so I look at it as more of a mini vacation. Since that man retired, he doesn't know what to do with himself."

"Awwww, maybe he just wants to spend time with his bestie."

"If his bestie is that saw in the garage, they sure do make a lot of noise."

Mr. Smith lowers his newspaper just below his eyes so he can see the two women talking back and forth. "I'm astonished at how you two are able to carry on like I'm not sitting right here."

"That's because even when you *are* here, you're not," says Mrs. Smith with a smile.

"Hey, Daddy. Good morning." Wendy kisses her dad on the cheek.

"Good morning, sweetie," he responds. "Now, for y'all's information, I have more than a great chance at getting this managerial job. And I'm making so much noise in there because I'm trying to help you stay afloat with your consignment shop."

"Help *me*?" Mrs. Smith asks.

"Yes, you know my unique pieces keep your shop going."

"If you say so," Mrs. Smith responds. "Are you done with your plate?"

"Yes, dear. Thank you for breakfast, and enjoy your day."

"Give me one more minute, Mom; these pancakes are everything right now," says Wendy.

"Girl, you need to come on … And thank you … I did put my foot in those blueberries."

😃

Wendy finishes her breakfast and the two women head out the door. Her mom kisses her father and they say "I love you" to each other.

"Bye, honey. Have a great day," Mr. Smith tells Wendy.

"Love you too, Dad," Wendy responds. "See you later."

***

Staring out of the airport window, Mark can't help but notice how gloomy and eerie the sky is looking. The clouds look gray and are moving very quickly. He's not the biggest fan of flying, but is anxious to get back to Wendy. They haven't seen each other for what seems like ages.

He turns his head to study the blue monitor, hoping his flight is on time. "Wendy would not be too happy with that," he says to himself. The last thing he needs is for her to be upset by a delay when he already has some news to talk to her about. He pulls his tablet out of his backpack and picks up where he left off on "Clash of Clans", a strategy game he has become borderline addicted to. After playing it for a while, he is relieved to hear an announcement regarding his flight.

"Flight 5799 Biloxi to Dallas Fort Worth now boarding groups 1 and 2. Please have your boarding pass and ID out as you make it to the front of the line," the American Airline announcer says.

Mark pulls his military ID out of his pocket, along with his boarding pass, checking it to make sure he is indeed part of group 1. He puts his tablet away and slides both arms into his new Air Force backpack. As he stands to walk, he stumbles slightly because his leg is a little numb from sitting for so long. He looks around, smiling, wondering if anybody else has noticed his fish legs.

Walking up to the line that starts at the reception desk, he glares at the 737 Boeing sitting right outside of the airport window. "Here we go again."

"Sir, boarding pass and ID, please," says the ticket agent.

"Sorry about that," Mark replies, "Here you go."

She scans the ticket, checks his ID, and sends him down the corridor to board the plane.

"Thank you for your service, sir, and have a great flight."

"Yes, ma'am. Thank you."

Walking down the corridor, Mark feels a hand touch his shoulder and as he looks to see who it is, an older gentleman with a black and yellow Vietnam hat also thanks him for his service.

"Thank you, sir. Thank you for your service also," Mark responds.

He's been getting used to the attention this uniform tends to bring. Approaching his window seat on the plane, he puts his backpack in the overhead bin and sits down to buckle up. After putting on his seatbelt and plugging in his headphones, he texts Wendy: **"I can't wait to see you."**

He knows she's asleep right now, but he thinks she'll be pleased to wake up to that message. As he stares out the window at the sky, he listens to some calming music. Laying his head between the wall of the plane and his seat, he's just comfortable enough to be able to fall asleep. *I can't wait to get back to Texas,* he thinks to himself as he's trying to nod off.

The plane finally takes off, giving Mark an intense feeling from being pushed back into his seat. After leveling off with the plane's ascension, Mark is able to doze off into much-needed sleep.

***

While on his second flight for the day, Mark is glad the trip from Dallas to San Antonio is not as lengthy as his flight from Biloxi. He's over flying right now. The clouds remind him of a fluffy pillow; he just wants to get home and relax. He doesn't even attempt to fall asleep on this flight, even though he's still pretty tired. Before he knows it, they've arrived at their destination. As soon as the plane pulls into the terminal, Mark turns on his phone. He feels multiple vibrations as the device boots up and sees that Wendy has been sending him messages.

"Are you here yet? Has the time changed? Hurry up and land the plane."

Smiling, he texts back, **"I'm here now."**

****

Wendy's phone beeps with a text message. "He's here!" she excitedly shouts to Mr. and Mrs. Johnson. Realizing how loud she's being in the middle of the airport, she laughs and apologizes to Mark's parents.

"I'm sorry. I'm just excited to get to see him again."

"You don't have to be sorry, sweetie," Mark's mother says. "We miss him, too. I just wish he'd call us more."

"You know how Mark is; he has to do his own thing," Mr. Johnson responds.

"Yeah, yeah, he's still my baby, regardless. Wendy, that is a beautiful dress, honey. Is that my second time saying that?" Mrs. Johnson laughs.

"No, it's only your third time, Mrs. Johnson," Wendy jokes.

12

"Girl, 😂 , it probably is, though. It's very beautiful, and Mark is very lucky."

Wendy blushes, "Awwwww, thank you. Wait … Is that him?" Wendy spots Mark out in a group people heading toward the baggage carousel in the airport.

Wendy takes off toward the arriving passengers in her yellow dress, trying not to run too fast because of her heels. She and Mark lock eyes and they both smile while holding each other tight and kissing.

"I missed you so much," Wendy whispers.

"I missed you too, babe," Mark replies.

He notices his parents looking at them and sees the tears in his mother's eyes from 20 feet away.

"I knew she was going to cry," he says with a grin. "I need to get home and get out of this uniform."

Wendy smiles at his remark. They walk over to his parents and Mark's mother immediately embraces him. "I've missed you so much," she says hugging him as tight as she can.

"Missed you too, Mom, even though it was only a few months," he answers with a grin.

"Oh, be quiet," Mrs. Johnson says.

Mark looks over at his father.

"Don't expect a hug from me, but it's good to see you, son," Mr. Johnson says.

The two men laugh, "I already know, Dad; good to see you too," Mark answers.

They hug anyway, and then wait for Mark's luggage before leaving the airport.

***

The next day, Mark wakes up to the comfort of his own bed. He hears the sink water running in the bathroom connected to his room. The last thing he remembers is drinking Air Force celebration shots with Wendy and not much after that. She exits the bathroom in one of his old t-shirts and heads straight over to kiss him. "I brushed my teeth so you wouldn't have to smell my morning breath."

Mark replies, "I still smell it. 😄 Just kidding."

"Haha... You've been gone for a while, but you still haven't improved your jokes, I see. But your chest has improved," Wendy says as she touches his left pec. "Have you been working out?"

"I have. You like?" Mark says while flexing with a serious look on his face.

"I do," she replies while winking and slightly biting her bottom lip.

The two bust out laughing and then discuss plans for the day. They decide to start out with breakfast and get dressed to head out the door to a local restaurant. Arriving to the mom-and-pop breakfast spot, Mark parks and hops of out the car to open Wendy's door for her. They walk in and are immediately greeted and taken to their seats. As they sit, the waitress approaches and takes their drink orders. Mark elects to have a coffee while Wendy chooses the orange juice.

As Mark looks out the restaurant window across the street at the old laundromat, he can't believe he's in the military; he feels Wendy's eyes piercing a hole in the side of his head. Without moving an inch, he asks her, "Why are you looking at me like that?"

"What are you thinking about?"

"Nothing...and everything at the same time."

😃

"It's not funny, Mark," she complains. "You've been gone like forever, and now you instantly have a look in your eye like you're stressed out. Is it about being here?"

"No, that's not it. It's not about me being here. It's just— nothing. I'm good."

"So, we just lie to each other now?" Wendy asks.

"No Wendy, it's..."

The waitress interrupts the two with their drinks and to take their order. Wendy decides she isn't hungry right now and asks for the waitress to come back.

Marks tells Wendy that he was ready to order.

"I'm ready for you to be honest with me," Wendy tells him.

"I'm not being stationed anywhere in Texas," Mark says.

"What? Then where?"

He braces himself as he finally tells her. "I'm going to New Jersey, to a base called McGuire."

"New Jersey????" Wendy repeats in confusion. "It doesn't matter. I'm going with you, or you're not going."

"It doesn't work like that, Wendy. I *have* to go," said Mark. "I can't really determine what happens in this career, you know that. I signed up for this with that understanding, and you knew what you were getting into."

Wendy looks at him with tears in her eyes. "I know, babe, but I still don't want to be without you. I have no idea what I'll do. I need you around more often."

"Are you ready to order?" the waitress stops by and asks again. Wendy and Mark pause their conversation to order their food. After ordering, they sit quietly for a few minutes from the uneasiness of the conversation they were having. It's like the cooks already knew what they wanted because the food arrived minutes later.

Mark starts to eat his scrambled eggs.

"Listen, Wendy, I know. I feel the same way. I'm bummed out with the way things are working out, I really am." Mark tries to comfort Wendy as best as he can, pulling her close to him in a supportive embrace. "But I'm done with basic training and tech school, so this next stop should be for a while. I really am sorry about all of these absences from class, Ms. Wendy!" He knows Wendy loves his silly side, and hopes the joke will lighten the mood.

"Stop playing." Wendy doesn't laugh. "This isn't funny. You're about to leave me again and you're making jokes about it! How can I come with you? There has to be a way."

"We can't have our girlfriends stay with us in the military dorm, Wendy," Mark says apologetically. "It's just not a realistic situation. I do know some buddies who got married because they wanted to bring their significant others along with them, but I don't know; maybe I can talk to somebody to see what the options are. I don't want to leave you here, and I also don't want to be out there by myself, either."

Mark's measured words don't have their intended effect on Wendy. "What do you mean, you don't know? If we can be together, wouldn't it be worth it? I'm beginning to think you're using this military housing situation as an excuse to get away from me."

"That's not true!" Mark protests, putting his hand over hers. "I love you, Wendy. I do, really. I just... I mean... I don't know. You think we're ready for marriage?" She pulls her hand away and folds her arms across her chest, glaring at him. "So you're just not going to answer me and let your food get cold?"

Wendy softens. "I'm ready for anything to be with you. If we're going to have a baby, what other choice do we have?"

Mark stops eating. "Baby…. *what?*"

She winks playfully, back to her usually joking self. "Got you! No, I'm not pregnant."

He exhales a huge sigh of relief. "Wow, that was your best joke ever, Wendy," he says sarcastically. "Okay, then. Either way, are you sure you're ready for marriage?"

"I'm ready for marriage and a baby. I'm not pregnant, but I wish I was. I want to have a little girl that looks just like me!" Wendy says bluntly.

"No way. We're going to have a boy that looks like me," Mark disagrees, somehow getting roped into a conversation about a baby they're not yet having.

"No way, my family has strong genes," Wendy threw back.

"Jeans, girl, I wear Levis! For real though, I'll look into it. I have a week to figure it out," Mark said.

She laces their fingers once more. "Thank you. I hope you know I don't mean to be a nag. I just miss you."

He squeezes her hand. "I know, babe. Me too."

"I mean, the courthouse is open on Monday, soooooo…"

Mark blinks in surprise and tilts his head a little, looking sideways at Wendy. "Uh, we'll see. Slow your roll. I just want to make sure everything is legit, okay? I have some calls to make, and I'll let you know how it could all work out. We can't just get married and show up at the base."

"Legit." Wendy hones in on that one word. "As in legit... legal... as in you're really considering it?"

Mark smiles. He loves this woman, impulsiveness and all. "Yeah. I'm considering it. Bigtime."

Wendy's jaw drops and she gazes into his eyes so lovingly, Mark knows he's made the right decision, regardless of how fast things suddenly have started moving.

TAKEAWAYS

Millennials can be abrupt when it comes to love. They can make a decision very quickly without giving the appropriate amount of thought to a situation. The military lifestyle does not make matters any simpler because the uncertainty of the occupation plays a part in decision-making. One day, a service member might be going to California, and the next, their orders could take them to another location on the other side of the country. This level of unpredictability makes couples uneasy, forcing them to consider a less than rational decision.

Based on what Mark has seen and heard from other military members, they feel that the only way to be together is if they get married. –*The Stigma*

2

NEWLYWEDS

"It's all so beautifulllll, relationships they seem from the start..."

-Bel Biv Devoe
"Poison"

Wendy and Mark get married! Mark figures out what he needs to do once he arrives at his base and receives the green light to make Wendy his bride. They have a small reception with a few friends and family at Wendy's church. It's quickly put together, but Wendy's family is friends with the pastor and he makes it happen for them on short notice.

Standing at the altar waiting for his wife to appear, Mark suddenly feels an intense sweat coming on. He uncomfortably adjusts his collar on his white rental suit. Looking down the large doorway of the church, he gets tunnel vision remembering the number of times he heard, "Are you sure about this?" This is the first time he felt any type of hesitation since they first discussed it a little over week ago. It all happened very quickly, but after discussing the decision in the breakfast joint that morning, Mark hasn't been able to imagine living without Wendy. He remembers that fact and stiffens his posture in a very confident, presentable manner as he has learned from the last few months in the military. Mark first sees a black dress shoe step around the corner and knows it's Wendy's father bringing her along. The next sight takes his breath away. Seeing his soon-to-be wife in that flawless white dress, everything escapes his mind and he can't think about anything except how beautiful she is.

Wendy takes the first step down the aisle and is immediately astonished with the way her husband looks in his suit. She has never seen him in a suit and she thinks he couldn't be more attractive. Excitement overwhelms her body and her legs have seemingly turned to Jell-O after the first few steps. She ganders a little at the crowd that has showed up and is amazed at what her mom was able to accomplish in such a short period of time. There are family members there she hasn't seen for a while, and she has a feeling of intense gratitude.

Approaching the altar, Wendy and Mark lock eyes and are unable to hold back the smile they both release. Going through the ceremony, both have short but very heartfelt vows. Mark mentions being away for military training and not being able to stop thinking about the woman he loves. Wendy speaks on how she felt Mark's love through the late night phone conversations she would fall asleep on. Both let it be known how deeply they are in love with each other and do not want to be apart any longer. Saying "I do" seems to eagerly come out of both of their mouths when the question is asked.

As they hold each other and passionately kiss in front of their families, Wendy's father jokingly says, "Okay, that's enough." As the church fills with laughter and joy, the ceremony is continued with a small dinner and light music. Mark and Wendy mingle with family and friends but can't wait to be alone. The night ends with them having champagne in the jacuzzi tub of their hotel room, enjoying each other without distractions. They finally got their wish to be alone and unbothered by anybody.

The next day, the two check out of the hotel, and head to the park on what seems to be a perfect day. As they walk down the park trail, Wendy jumps up and down with excitement. "Oh my God, babe; I can't believe we did it! I love you so much! My mom says we should definitely look into buying a house since we're in a decent housing market, but before, we need to plan a cruise for our honeymoon, or maybe even go to the Bahamas or something! I think we…"

Mark looks into the distance at a woman jogging toward

them with a large dog running beside her. Trying to guess the breed, initially he doesn't register what Wendy is saying. His eyes grow wide as he catches up fast.

"Whoa." Mark grabs Wendy by the waist and takes her hand in his, looking at his beautiful new bride. "Wendy, slow down for a second. We're getting pretty far ahead of ourselves, don't you think?"

Her smile fades, Mark notices, and he holds back a sigh. Mark wants to make his wife happy, but he also wants to do it on their terms, not on her mother's every suggestion.

"A house? The Bahamas? Your mom isn't paying for that, is she? We need to be conservative right now. We still have to get to the base and do things appropriately with paperwork and registration and all that so I can officially move off-base. We have to find somewhere to live and everything."

Wendy turns and resumes walking, letting go of Mark's hands. "I know, I know; we have to do this, we have to do that. My mom is just making sure we get started the right way. We obviously have a lot to do, so why can't you just focus on us for right now?"

Mark admires her long, shapely legs, becoming briefly distracted until Wendy turns and raises her eyebrows.

"Mark, did you hear me?"

"Uh, I am. I mean, I did," he replies hastily. "Yes, I am focused on us, but the military is going to be our livelihood for the next four years *at least*," he emphasizes. "You don't have an income right now, and we need to be able to have basic necessities before we go splurging on things. I just want us to be comfortable both now and later, honey. Spending our meager savings right now isn't practical."

It's obvious that Wendy doesn't see his practical take on the situation. "So, our marriage is a splurge to you? We only need to have one honeymoon."

"That's not what I'm saying." He tries again. "We just have to make sure we do things right, that's all. When we get settled, it's just going to be the two of us. We're not going to have any family around to help us, just me and you."

Wendy shakes her head, her eyes like fire as she turns away again. "All right. Whatever... I guess we just won't celebrate our marriage."

:(

"Are you for real? Come here." Mark takes a couple quick steps to catch up and pulls his wife close to him. "You don't have to make me feel bad. I just want to make sure we're going to be taken care of. I don't wanna struggle; I had enough of that before joining the military."

"We're not going to struggle," Wendy replies, leaning closer into him. "The military pays you on the first and the fifteenth every month. My mom was dating a military guy before Dad, and she said the steady paycheck could really help us. They pay no matter what on the first and the fifteenth, so you're good for the next four years, right?" She looks up into his eyes with a puppy dog smile.

"Yeah, no…" It's hard to resist the look, but he tries. "That doesn't necessarily mean we're good. We just have to be able to maintain. If we get into a hole, the military won't pay me more just to get out of it. We have to find an apartment, a car; I just want to get settled and make sure we get taken care of. That can't be too much to ask, right? Like I said, it's just going to be us. I just want to start things off the right way."

Wendy has always tended to be much more optimistic than Mark. She squeals, "We're officially married, so we've already started off the right way!"

Mark hears footsteps trotting toward him and knows it's the lady with the dog. He turns to watch her approach, still trying to figure out the breed. As she gets closer, he says out loud, "Beethoven!"

The lady looks at him and smiles as she passes the couple, barely controlling the enormous animal as it bounds ahead, tugging at its leash.

"Beethoven?" Wendy asks in confusion.

"I've been looking at that dog trying to figure out the breed," Mark explains. "I just realized it's a St. Bernard, like the dog movie."

Wendy laughs and leans up to kiss his cheek. "Strange man. Now, what about this honeymoon? Would you like to take the dog with us? We'll have to buy him an extra ticket or two, so not exactly conservative."

Mark chuckles but can't help but to give into his beautiful wife, "You're right. Let's plan for a romantic getaway after we get all moved in and settled. How does that sound? I promise it'll be worth the wait!"

Wendy can't contain her excitement and dances with delight. "Let's do that! I'd like a hotel suite on the water, champagne, a five-star restaurant, and definitely a spa before that! Sound modest enough?"

"Yeah, that's definitely a modest approach," Mark hedges.

😌

He wants to give her all her dreams, but can't help but worry about exactly how things are going to fall into place.

TAKEAWAYS

The newlywed stage brings forth an abundant amount of excitement. There sometimes tends to be one individual in the relationship who is looking to be a little more conservative about laying the marital foundations, whereas the other wants to do everything right here and now. Who can blame either party in this scenario? In many military relationships, the couple can be hundreds of miles away from their family and friends. They're journeying into a new life together, both diving headfirst into the unknown.

In Mark and Wendy's case, this is the first time Wendy will ever be away from her family. She has a very close relationship with her mother and now her life has almost instantly changed by getting married, moving away, and being outside of her comfort zone. This couple is now relying solely on each other, and it's their responsibility to build their life with the knowledge and wisdom they've acquired thus far. Being in their early twenties, the task will be a tall order, but the two are deeply in love. They will need to be cognizant of each other's feelings and perceptions from here on out. Understanding is everything.

3

BABY BUMP

"Like a baseball field, wanna hit a homerun
Me and you get together, babe, and raise a little one..."

-R. Kelly
"Half on a Baby"

Two weeks in the base hotel wasn't ideal for either one of them, although they did have housekeeping when they needed it; that was a plus for Wendy who was frequently requesting for Mark to pick up his things. She's not used to cleaning up after somebody else. Luckily, they find an apartment off the base before too long. They had the assistance of the housing office to help facilitate that for them. Seeing how things work in the military gave Wendy an idea of what Mark was getting into with his career choice.

Wendy and Mark settle into a place close to their new military base, McGuire AFB. It's a nice apartment complex that has a small fitness center on site, a park for kids, and a dog park. Because of the park, they almost immediately have a conversation regarding a pet. "Chihuahua, please," is all Mark remembers Wendy saying during that conversation.

It takes them both a little while to get settled into their new environment learning a little more each day as the time passes. After two more semesters of Wendy's schooling, she completes her nursing degree. This is a huge accomplishment for her and brings about conversations on expanding the family. That has been an ongoing discussion since they've been married for the last 7 months, but now it's getting more serious given the amount of time that has passed without positive results. That has brought about challenges for Mark while he gets acclimated to the demands of the military lifestyle. It's hard on both of them, being away from friends and family while creating their new life together, but they're adjusting.

"You're gonna hear me rooooarrrrr..." Wendy's phone plays a Katy Perry ringtone as she sings along in the mirror while putting her long brown hair in a ponytail. She looks down to see who it is and there's a picture of her mom with a big smile on her face.

She picks the phone up after finishing her hair. "Hey, Mom."

"So, are you all ready to give me my grandbabies yet? I'm not getting any younger, you know."

Wendy rolls her eyes. "Mommmmmm, I think that's the *only* reason you call me. How about, *'How are you doing, Wendy?'* That would be a good conversation starter, right?"

"No idea who you're talking to like that, but if you must know, yes, that's the only reason I call." Wendy's mom laughs.

"Be quiet. I don't know though, Mom, it feels awkward talking to you about this, but I think Mark needs to get a sperm count done. We've been trying ever since we got here. Literally like every day possible."

"Girl, I asked you if you were pregnant, not if you all were getting it on! Ugh! But yeah, I agree. Maybe he needs to see what is wrong with his little swimmers. He did used to smoke a lot of pot, didn't he? Killing that poor sperm."

Wendy remembers in high school when her mom would tease her about Mark getting caught smoking pot in their senior year. "Pot can really lower your sperm count?" Wendy asks.

"How am I supposed to know? You're the nurse! I'm just assuming that could be the problem."

She rolls her eyes. "You're something else, Mom, but we'll figure it out. I really miss you guys. Being away from home is different; it's hard."

"We miss you too, sweetie."

"Tell Daddy I love him. I haven't talked to him in ages. I know he wasn't completely happy with me getting married so fast, I'm just glad he was cordial and supported me." Wendy feels a tug of sadness, hating the slight rift between her and her father.

"Then call him if you want to talk to him."

"The phone works both ways," she says stubbornly. "But I'll call him soon."

"Mark will be home shortly. I'll call you back later. I love you."

"Love you, too. Now get busy making those babies!"

***

Mark pulls up to the apartment in their 2010 black Acura. He looks at the window that leads to the living room of the apartment and once again notices the blind that has been bent for a while to allow someone to see through at that spot in the window. He thinks to himself, "I have to get some more blinds," and as soon as the thought passes, he feels his exhaustion telling him, *not today*. He grabs his camouflage Air Force backpack and gets out of the car.

Mark walks through the door and sees his wife lying down watching TV instead of coming to greet him as she usually does when she hears him arrive. "Hey, what's going on? How was your day?"

"Well, I've been stuck in this apartment all day, bored out of my mind, and still not pregnant with my baby. How do you think it went?" Wendy snaps.

"Okay..." The last thing he wants to do is fight. "That's great. Remind me not to ask you about your day anymore. It's been a long day at work. I just want to eat, shower, and chill without arguing. Did you make anything?."

Wendy snaps again, "Have *you* made anything? It seems like both ovens are empty around here, huh?"

Mark looks at Wendy with a puzzled expression. "Are you serious right now? I'm tired, Wendy. I've been at work all day. And why do you continue insinuating that I'm the reason you're not getting pregnant? How do we know it's not issues with you?"

He's admittedly surprised at how his wife is acting over something that he views to be a non-issue. He looks at the matter with the mentality, *it'll happen when it's supposed to; we just have to be patient.*

"I'm not the one who spent my youth smoking weed. You need to see a doctor or something," she accuses.

Mark stares at her in disbelief. "I'm definitely fertile, okay? *You* should see a doctor because I know I'm good. And I'm too hungry and tired to discuss this. Let's just go get some McDonald's or something." He doesn't understand why she's getting so worked up over this. And why do they have to have a baby immediately, anyway? It seems like they just got married!

Wendy rises to her feet from the couch and crosses her arms defiantly. "What!? How the hell you know you're *definitely good*? You got some kids I don't know about or something?" She says this in a sarcastically serious manner.

Looking through the refrigerator, Mark replies, "No, none of that. I can just feel it inside me."

Wendy gets a little louder, "Okay, keep thinking it's funny. I'm gonna have a baby!"

"And I don't doubt that. But let's talk about this later, because again, I'm just tired… And hungry." There is nothing in the fridge.

"I don't care what you are. You need to make sure you schedule that appointment…" Wendy insists.

Mark marshals his temper and turns to her. "Listen, everything's going to be fine, all right? How do we know you're not pregnant right now? Because with all these emotions you're throwing around—"

Wendy cuts Mark off in the middle of his sentence, "Stop playing with me, okay!? I'm not being emotional! I just want you to get your sperm count checked!"

"Wendy, I love you," he sighs.

"If you did, you'd get checked," she insists, rolling her eyes.

"Okay, we can try to schedule something, all right? I'll do it for you." Mark caves in, just to stave off a fight.

"See how easy that was? Thank you. Now go get us some McDonald's..."

Mark kisses his wife on the cheek while her arms are still crossed. He grabs the keys and her hand and gently pulls her outside so they can go get food together.

***

Five months later, the two finally end up accomplishing their goal and find out Wendy is pregnant. Mark is thrilled his trip to the doctor reveals a normal sperm count, and equally happy to be a father-in-waiting. Wisely, he kept to himself the fact that Wendy pushed very hard for him to get checked, putting the delay on his shoulders. But it seemed their pregnancy issue was merely a matter of time, because there was no circumstance-changing action that took place aside from the visit to the doctor. Wendy is on Cloud 9 with the news and it has definitely created a much happier atmosphere; however, the two are still conscious about the way they bumped heads along the way to reach this point.

TAKEAWAYS

Having a baby can be a highly sensitive situation for many people. In a young marriage where the couple is actively trying to conceive a child, both individuals have to consider how the other feels about the matter. In this scenario, Mark is relaxed about everything while Wendy is very focused on making it happen. They both need to look at the situation from each other's perspective and thereby avoid situations that get blown out of proportion. Truly understanding how badly Wendy wants to have a child can help Mark empathize and be more patient with her feelings. Having baby fever made her very emotional. With this, Wendy must also practice empathy because it was perceivably nobody's fault for the amount of time it was taking for her to get pregnant. The eagerness she was experiencing made her feel like time was quickly passing by, which played a role in her emotional state. In this phase of marriage, people are very susceptible to behaving in an uncharacteristic manner, especially when dealing with such a sensitive subject. Again, *empathy* is the key factor here.

4

GLORY DAYS

"Everything is awesomeeeeee,
When you're living out a dream..."

-The Lego Movie
"Everything is Awesome"

Ten months later, Mark and Wendy finally have their bundle of joy! This just as exciting as when they were newlyweds. The addition of a baby makes everything in life simultaneously cute and cautious. Everything the baby does seems to be the cutest thing ever and when he sleeps, Wendy is susceptible to checking to make sure he is breathing. Family trips to the zoo and aquarium are great first-time experiences and more than enough pictures are always taken.

Mark has gone away a couple times for training here and there on a temporary duty assignment (TDY). A temporary duty station used for training can be a requirement under the member's particular career field, giving them no choice but to attend. On his most recent one, he had the opportunity to bring his family along with him. While gone on the TDY, the young family has a great time and they are still reminiscing about it a couple months later.

Scrolling through the pictures they'd taken, Wendy exclaims, "That trip was everything! It was sooooo beautiful! We need to plan another one soon. Little Mark is definitely going to have a nice collage of where he's been. I'm 23 years old and this kid has literally been to as many places as I have! That's amazing." Wendy has a wide smile, watching Little Mark play with his Jumbo Legos on their tan area rug.

"It really is. That's one thing the military provides, I guess. A chance to see more of the world. I know people back home who have barely even left the city. That place is like a black hole," Mark chuckles. "But it was awesome to see the Grand Canyon. I never even imagined going there at all. It was quite an experience." Mark loves that he could share the trip with his family. His father stayed in Texas for most of his career, so he's not a typical military brat who's been all over.

"Quite an experience? Haha! Since when did you start talking like that? All proper and whatnot." Wendy teases.

"And whatnot? You sound like a little old lady yourself."

😄

"Whatever." Wendy scrolls through her pictures on her phone and starts clicking through her social media. "My mom said the pictures we took were really nice; she said she's happy for us making it this far in our marriage." Wendy lifts her head from her white iPhone and adds, "And of course she would put that on the Facebook post."

"Making it this far? What's she expecting, for us to not make it?" Mark asks, not exactly thrilled at the news.

"No, just making it this far as a couple, I guess." Wendy shrugs, "You know how popular divorce is nowadays. All Mom watches is her Lifetime Channel..."

"I mean, do you two talk about us splitting up or something? What do you talk about?" he presses.

"No, we don't talk about us splitting up," Wendy replies as she rolls her eyes. "My mom talks about a thousand things. What Dad is doing, what my sisters have been up to, how well we are doing with Mark... She also mentions Little Mark getting a little brother one day."

Wendy giggles a little bit but she has a playfully serious vibe. With the way she made that statement sound like a question,

Mark can sense Wendy is having thoughts about another baby.

He responds, "I think if Mrs. Johnson wants us to have another baby, she's going to have to take care of those 'other baby' expenses."

Wendy raises an eyebrow, her good mood halfway fading. "Don't talk about my mom, okay?"

"What?" Mark says, "You brought her up."

Luckily, Wendy seems to momentarily let go of whatever bugged her. "She's just super happy about Little Mark because she's finally a grandmother. Now she can stay off my back about us getting it on."

"Huh? Getting it on?" Mark goes a little green. "You talk to your mom about us having sex?"

"Ugh! NO!" Wendy exclaims. "I'm just saying, she was just as anxious as I was for us to have a baby... Honestly, it was kind of weird. Enough about our conversations. But don't you think it's about time to go ahead and start talking about another one though? A sibling for our little man? I don't want to be old and having more kids."

Her hopeful expression tells him she definitely isn't kidding and Mark takes his time before he speaks. "We can talk about it. But I don't think we're ready at this moment to have another. We are really *just* getting settled in; you're settling into your new role with the hospital; I'm settling in well with the military."

As Mark rambles off excuses to wait on having another baby, Wendy has already tuned him out.

She responds, "I've been at my job for over a year. We've been living on base what seems like forever, and I'm definitely not getting any younger."

"Wendy, I really think we should take our time with this. Little Mark's not even a year," he begins. "And when was the last time we were able to spend quality time together as a couple? If we had a baby right now, we'd be adding more responsibility and less time for us."

"Well, first off," Wendy counters, "We can't just say let's have a baby and it'll be here tomorrow. It takes over nine months for a baby to get here once you're pregnant."

Mark shakes his head. "We got pregnant when we were supposed to the first time. There was nothing wrong with either one of us. And it was a blessing to be able to get into base housing before the baby came. Imagine moving like we did with a tiny newborn and a toddler, because we don't know when a PCS is coming."

"It's not like I helped. I was coming due and I literally did a minimal amount of helping with that. I think I could handle another minimal participation move."

"You were up walking around and helped direct the movers. That's help to me," Mark answers, not being too serious. "And

I'm just referring to having a newborn and a toddler trying to make that type of move happen. It would be even more stressful."

Both Wendy and Mark sit in silence for a few minutes, watching Little Mark now play with his favorite Tonka truck and watch Sesame Street simultaneously.

Wendy speaks softly. "If we get pregnant by the time Little Mark turns two, the baby can be here by the time he's three. He's already in daycare, and he'll be out of diapers by then."

"You just started back working what seems like yesterday," Mark replies. "And now you want to get pregnant, and in a few months be out of work again? That soon?"

"It's more than a few months," she says.

"Sure…" Mark replies. "You know, since the baby has been here, we haven't really spent much time together at all. No *you and me* time. Once we add another child into the mix, that's more attention that needs to be spread out and taken away from each other."

"So, you believe another child is going to tear us apart?" Wendy asks.

"That's not what I'm saying at all," he replies, "but I care about *us* and our relationship as much as I care about building a family together. It's been just us this whole time and we haven't really had anybody to help us with anything. Taking care of the baby, working, no date nights, nothing. I'm just saying, another baby is going to make it that much more difficult to do those things."

Wendy doesn't completely understand where Mark is coming from. She wants to build their family and she feels that the family is strength enough to get them through anything. She gets the date nights and time spent together, but she sees time out as a family as the same type of bonding period for the two of them.

"We can do things as a family like we *just* did with your trip."

"I agree, but don't you think we need *you and me* time to focus on each other?" Mark reasons.

"We could have had you and me time if we would have taken our honeymoon like you promised, but that didn't happen." Wendy still remembers the conversation regarding their honeymoon that never happened. She hasn't fully forgiven Mark for the broken agreement. "Sure, just make excuses like you always do to keep from agreeing with me on something important."

"That's not it, and you know it," he retorts, starting to lose his patience. "Just be realistic."

"I am!" Wendy snaps.

"How!? You literally are trying *not* to see my point of view!" Mark barks.

"And you're trying so hard to see mine, right!? You always do! Right?"

Little Mark turns away from Elmo singing a song and gazes toward the loud voices while still holding his toy truck. Mark notices this and gets uneasy at his son watching them.

He caves in. "Okay, Wendy. You're right, like usual."

"Like usual? What you mean like usual? Huh?" Wendy yells.

He gives up and gets up. "You're always right, I'm always wrong; that's what I mean."

"Okay. That settles it, then. We're having a baby again."

"Man, you're something else." Mark walks out of the room, saying, "We can continue this discussion when you're more receptive to actually understanding things that make sense. Does that sound fair?"

"Does that sound fair? How about you just be quiet and get ready for another baby. Does that sound fair?" she snipes.

"Sure it does, Wendy, sure it does." Mark walks from the living area to their dimly lit bedroom. He sits on their queen-sized bed, staring at his black dresser, contemplating changing clothes to go to the gym. He focuses his eyes on the hallway that leads back to the living room and shakes his head at what just happened.

Not liking how the conversation ended, Wendy shortly makes her way into the room after Mark, and sits on the bed next to him. She grabs his hand and squeezes it tight enough to show her care and concern. Mark is reluctant at giving into the gesture, but eventually tightens his loose grip. Wendy tilts her head, laying it on his shoulder. The two remain in the same position for several moments, not saying a word. It's implied that both felt the same regret for their interaction.

TAKEAWAYS

In a marriage, there are still two different individuals with two different mindsets coming together to live life with each other. That's not a simple challenge by any means. The first couple of years will seem to fly by, but also stand still at times. When you're having fun, time flies, but when things are tough, life can seem stagnant. Mark and Wendy are content with their married life, but they still have some different ideas about things that are just surfacing. The toughest situations arise when one person feels very deeply about something and the other does not view the matter in the same light. Mark is thinking of stability while Wendy is thinking of completing their family. Neither is really wrong in their respective ideas or desires, but getting on the same page is pivotal at this point. Sitting down and writing out what each individual's wants/needs are can be a start to getting on the same page and understanding one another.

Wendy's parents have been married for over 20 years. Growing up, she recognized how her parents never finished the day on bad terms. This is a great standard Millennials can learn from previous generations. When ending the day on bad terms, you're more susceptible to waking up on bad terms. Always make amends before the day ends.

5

WHO ARE YOU?

"I realize when it comes to girls that chemistry
Means way more than anatomy, she mad at me..."

-Big Sean
"Halfway off the Balcony"

Lately, Wendy has been getting frustrated with her job. It's just not everything she had hoped it would be. She has thoughts of her grandmother being the reason she got into the career field. It saddens her remembering the lack of attention her grandmother received in her last days. Her vision of helping people hasn't translated into her reality, though; working in a clinic isn't her idea of giving back to people. She is now faced with working full-time doing something she thought she would love, and then going home to take care of the house, too. It's starting to get a little overwhelming.

Driving down a slightly foggy road, Wendy looks ahead at what looks like endless brake lights. On this particular morning, the weather doesn't look great outside, but her car is nice and warm, making her a little sleepy. Slowing down while getting closer to the stopped vehicles, she calls her mom, trying to stay awake on her way to work. Wendy feels reluctant to vent, but she knows it's going to happen. Utilizing her voice command Bluetooth in the recently acquired Ford Escape, Wendy says, "Call Mom." She listens to the phone ring while holding her head in her hand and staring at the red light.

Mrs. Johnson answers the phone on the first ring. "Hey, baby, how are you today?"

Knowing her mom was going to answer the phone rather quickly, Wendy speaks honestly, "Hey, Mom, I've been better. This job is really getting on my nerves. Why don't you go to work for me today?"

"Yeah, no," her mom teases, like she always does when trying to lift Wendy's spirits. "I'm no longer equipped to deal with that type of responsibility. I'm enjoying life running my shop. Besides, raising you kids was work enough! That's why I didn't have a steady job when you were growing up. I let your daddy bring home the bacon, lol."

Wendy manages to smile. "Sorry, I forgot how they did things in the '60s," she jokes.

"You watch your mouth. 😄 I was born in the '70s, for your information. But you're not liking it, though? Why don't you find another job?"

"It's not that I don't like it," Wendy replies. "It's just the same old thing every day. Work, go home and take care of the house and Little Mark while Mark does his thing. He and I." Wendy hesitates while speaking as the traffic moves and she drives through the green light. She continues, "We're just not as good as we're supposed to be. Marriage is hard," Wendy admits sadly. Unfortunately, the two have experienced even more challenges.

"You're right, it is, but it's not supposed to be easy. Would it be worth it if it was? You have a good man in Mark, though... Don't you? I'm sure he understands, *happy wife, happy life*."

"That's the last thing he understands," Wendy scoffs. "But hey, I have to go in now ,so I'll call you on lunch or something."

"Does Little Mark have plans for a playmate yet?" her mother presses.

"Take a wild guess. 😑 I just want to get my babies out of the way while I'm still young... Oh well. Love you, Mom."

"I understand that! But don't worry Wendy, things will be

fine. Love you too, baby. Enjoy your day."

Wendy arrives at work and settles in. It doesn't feel great outside, but her clinic always has a different type of chill in the air. She puts on her handy, faded green scrub top with long sleeves to deal with the cold environment. Still frustrated about her situation at home, she looks up after putting on her jacket to see somebody walking to her desk.

Her supervisor, Jody, is a friendly, good-looking guy and can see that she is in distress. He swoops over with a big grin on his face and leans on the side of her desk. "Hey, how's your day going, Wendy?"

"It's okay. I've obviously had better, though, especially since we're all being micromanaged, right?" Wendy groans.

"Ha ha, no you're not being micromanaged. I'm just here to report back everything I see." He says playfully.

"Whatever, be quiet."

"There it is! I haven't witnessed a laugh from this area of the office in a while." He leans in closer.

"Please don't worry about this side of the room and the laughter that comes from it." She tries to hold back her smile but can't help it because it's nice to have the attention.

"Are you good, though? How's life treating you?" he asks.

"Well... it's... um, it's been better, really. After work, I have to go home and get right back to work. And being here makes me feel out of place sometimes because it's not always easy working with other women and some of their snobbiness."

"They're fine with me," he comments.

☺

"You get along with them because they like you. I'm a female office competitor or whatever, so I don't get googly eyes, I get batted eyelids." She flirts with him in an overly exaggerated display.

He smiles. "Now that's a funny way to put it. But seriously? I get googly eyes? From who? Michelle, Janice, don't tell me… Robin? Ugh…" His eyes search the clinic, trying to see who is crushing on him.

Wendy laughs and responds, "You're mean, and you know what I'm saying."

"Yeah, yeah. Hey, but honestly, you seem like you could use a little boost to get through this day," he says. "How about you let me buy you a coffee?"

"Three creams, two sugars; hazelnut is fine."

"Wow," he grins, "I like when a woman knows what she wants..."

"Mmm-hmm. I'm sure you do. Coffee, please, and thanks." A sly smile creeps over Wendy's lips. She secretly likes her supervisor being sweet on her. It's a nice break from her marriage difficulties where the main communication seems to be through arguments.

"Yes, ma'am, no problem. I'll be back shortly." He whisks away on his mission to get Wendy's coffee, then turns back around a few feet away from her desk to flash his bright white smile, batting his eyelids in mockery of what she just did. Playing along, she blushes and looks away, giggling inside like a little schoolgirl.

Wendy looks at her computer's blue screen and sees a list full of patients for the day. With a deep exhale, she softly says to herself, "How can the schedule be this full on a Monday..."

***

Mark parks in his usual parking space after finishing up a game of football with his military buddies following work. He's in his favorite gray sweats and holding his dirt filled cleats in one hand. He tries slamming them on the pavement a few times to get all of the dirt off, but doesn't notice his poor effort on the cleats before heading to the front door. Walking in, he drops the cleats by the front door as he always does. When he drops them, some dry dirt particles fall onto the floor.

Mark grabs his back in pain. "Dang, my back hurts." He leans over and picks up his son, who has gotten much better at walking over the last few weeks. Mark kisses his son's cheek, neck, and forehead, then lightly tickles him through his blue Thomas the Train onesie. "Hey, buddy, how's it going? Daddy missed you! Missed you too, Mommy; how was your day?"

Mark sees that Wendy looks a little frustrated while sweeping the kitchen, but seeing her frustration never keeps him from interacting with her.

She answers him, "Stop, I'm trying to clean up this mess." Wendy is visibly irate as she makes her way to the front door to sweep up the dirt around his shoes instead of greeting him.

"Stop what? I'm just trying to say hi after not seeing you all day." Mark is starting to expect some coldness at times, but it isn't something he can get used to. He recognizes Wendy starting to sweep around his cleats. He puts Little Mark down and grabs the shoes to take them back outside to clean them off a little more.

As he picks them up, Wendy says, "You literally disregard me because you dropped those filthy cleats on my floor once again. And you're right, you didn't see me... But you also didn't text me, didn't call me, or anything else. You weren't thinking about me." She turns her back to Mark and continues to sweep the floor.

"Listen, I apologize for the cleats. That was not my intent. But the phone, that goes both ways, right?" Mark answers, following behind her. "Because my phone didn't go off, either. What's up with you? I can't come in and say hi to my wife and get some love back?" This has now become an unfortunate routine. He'll say something he considers loving and get snapped at in return for a mistake he didn't realize he made. Although, he does see how the cleats made her upset.

"Come here," Wendy says. She walks up to Mark and swiftly kisses him in a meaningless manner. "Are you happy? Now you can go do some more stuff that has nothing to do with me, like playing football with your buddies."

"Aww, come onnnn... Now, I told you, I do apologize for those cleats, but what am I doing to deserve this treatment?" Mark stares at her. "All I do is work, play football, come home, spend time with you all, and then when you go to sleep, I stay up late doing homework. I'm pursuing this degree to become an officer and help us make more money. And you are being unappreciative of that... I make a direct effort to spend time with you two."

All Mark knows is that he's trying to do his best with everything right now; to fit family, his military duties, school, friends, and everything else into one day.

"That's right, *you two*! We still haven't had another conversation about another baby!" Wendy yells.

Mark grabs his son and takes him into his room down the hall to get him away from the discussion he knows is looming. He sits him on his ABC rug, turns his TV on, and clicks play on his *Little Einsteins* DVD.

Walking back to the living room, Mark already knows what

MILLENNIAL MARRIAGES - "A MILITARY RELATIONSHIP"

he is going to say. "Wendy, can we please stay on one subject!? So, the reason you've been acting like this is because you want another baby right now?! Because I didn't text or call you all day? Or is it because I'm doing too many things that don't involve you? You're everywhere with this; you don't even know what you're mad at!" Mark feels like nothing is ever good enough for his wife.

"I'm just tired of it!" she screams. "You don't think about me! You only think about yourself!" Wendy throws the broom down on the kitchen floor in anger and storms toward their bedroom.

Mark heads back toward his son's room. He approaches Little Mark, kisses him on his head, and whispers, "Love you, buddy."

Little Mark is drawn to his cartoons, so he really doesn't even budge. Mark walks into his and Wendy's bedroom.

He sees Wendy lying on the bed with her phone in her hand, looking as angry as she could possibly look. "Listen," he starts off, "I come in trying to kiss you and greet you and all I want is for you to do the same. This is ridiculous. Let's not do this right now. We need to talk like we have some sense." Mark is having trouble figuring out how to fix things because she has so many grievances, he doesn't even know where to start.

"That's one thing we can agree on. I'm about to go to the store," she informs him.

"For what?" he says in surprise.

"I'm getting some wine... And I need some money for it. You

55

want to know anything else?" She puts her hand out, demanding cash with a pissed-off look in her eyes.

Mark answers, "You don't have a job? Never mind, here." He reluctantly pulls out his wallet and gives her his USAA debit card.

As Wendy takes the card, she simultaneously turns to walk out of the room. Standing there frustrated with mixed emotions, Mark hears the front door slam. He feels the conversation has not ended yet. He pulls his iPhone out of his pocket and starts to send Wendy a text.

While angrily texting, Mark sees a figure in his doorway. He raises his eyes from his phone to see his son walking to him, saying, "Dada."

Mark looks at the phone and realizes the terrible things he was about to send. He sets his phone on the dresser, grateful to have this unconditional love.

TAKEAWAYS

This phase is called "Who Are You" because the two are each starting to show where their priorities lie. They have been learning more and more about the perceived values of their spouse. Both individuals should know they have to change their lifestyle in a marriage; it's not just them being able to solely focus on themselves anymore. They've also brought a child into the world, so they're forced to keep that in mind when going through the struggles or making decisions that could have an impact on the family. The problem here is there was never really a solid foundation of values or principals that were established for the relationship.

A difficult aspect of getting married at a young age is trying to figure out who you are as a person while simultaneously trying to figure somebody else out. We all typically grow in some form or another, but the objective should be to grow *together*.

Open communication is essential in a marriage. If Wendy is having issues with Mark spending a lot of time out of the house, she should let him know her grievance in a rational manner. This will make him more willing to try to understand how she feels. He could also tactfully ask her what's going on. The inability to do this has led them to a terrible place as a couple and has made Wendy vulnerable to outside attention. Everybody works with a guy that I like to call "Mr. Friendly." There's one in every work center, and they tend to be extremely friendly, charming, helpful, etc. It's like they can detect a woman in distress because they're the ones always coming to the rescue, attempting to make them smile or laugh during trying times. If Wendy doesn't remain aware and get what she needs from home, it could have a very detrimental impact on their marriage.

At the end of the interaction with his wife, Mark learns something very important. He learns that when you're grateful for something, it's hard to remain angry. When Little Mark comes to him in the middle of his frustrated text, he realizes what he's doing and how it's not worth it. My advice in times of anger would be to try to focus on what you're grateful for. Especially if you have kids, you'll be able to quickly realize how unimportant the anger really is. When it gets hard, remember your blessings.

6

RESPECT MUCH?!

*"Some of them men think they freak this
Like we do, but no they don't
Make your check, come at they neck
Disrespect us, no they won't..."*

**-Beyoncé
"Run the World (Girls)"**

"Game!" Mark yells as the basketball falls through the white net. His co-worker and friend, Lance, gives him a high five on their way to the water fountain.

"Good shot, man," Lance says. They walk through the large double doors of the base gym and stand in line for the fountain.

"You playing again?"

"Nah, I'm exhausted, man," Mark replies. "Plus, I need to hurry up and get home so I don't get my head bitten off."

😄 "What you talking about, man?"

"I'm talking about my wife, bro. She's been having more and more issues with me playing sports or just being out of the house altogether. I remember when she used to encourage me to go to all my games to get out the house. Not anymore. All she does now is just complain about it," Mark answers.

"Oh, so you're serious?" Lance asks. "I thought you were just messing with me."

They walk back through the double doors after getting some water. Sitting down on the metal bleachers by their gym bags, they continue the conversation.

"You better hurry up and get home!" Lance laughs.

"Bro, I seriously don't know what to do. We haven't been getting along at all and I have no idea what the reason is. I've been sending flowers, making dinner, massaging... all kinds of stuff."

Lance responds, "Let me ask you something. When you're massaging, do you end up having sex every time, too?" Lance can't help but ask this question with a huge smile on his face.

Mark answers, "Man, I thought I was the only one doing that. I mean, I feel like it's just the next logical step."

The two laugh hysterically for a few seconds. Finally, Lance responds, "You're definitely not alone on that note. But yeah, I know you've been sending flowers and all that junk. I don't hear enough of it! That's all my wife says to me for real, 'Wendy said Mark did this, Mark did that, blah blah...' I just sit there and think, 'We need to stop hanging out with Mark and them, huh?'"

Lance is one of Mark's co-workers and their families have started to spend a little time together. Lance also has a young child around the same age as Little Mark, which is an added bonus for their friendship. Being miles away from their families, they've discovered that military friendships can turn out to be sort of a family away from family.

Mark responds, "Stop hanging out?" He laughs. "Man, no! Then I'd really go crazy! Tell me, if it really is like that, how do you explain the way she's been acting? She's been talking crazy to me! I get tired of the disrespect. I must be wasting my money on these flowers." Mark shakes his head in disbelief.

"I don't know, man. I get some craziness here and there, too," Lance says, "but I'm not doing all the things you're doing. You seem like a machine man. School, work, sports, husband, father, volunteer work, like when do you sleep?"

"I don't. I'm a beast, man," Mark smiles. "Nah, I manage; school isn't a big deal, I just do it when everybody in the house goes to sleep. Sports are life, work is work, and the family gets most of my evenings. At least the ones that you aren't trying to play 'Call of Duty' online 24/7!" Mark laughs at his own statement.

"I don't know, it might help your relationship. Maybe your wife would like for you to be a full-blown gamer and just sit at home all the time. Just a thought." Lance shrugs.

"I can't just stay in the house like that. Heck, no. But get this, she wants to have another baby, like really soon. At first I thought we were past the request, but it keeps coming back up," Mark tells his friend. "I really think she despises me because I'm not fully on board with just having a second child immediately. She wants an exact date for planning purposes," Mark shakes his head.

"Well, that might be the issue. She wants the bun in the oven, and you've cut back on your carbs. Good one, right?" Lance jokes.

"Nah, not really; you're not that funny, bro," Mark laughs anyway. "Seriously though, this marriage stuff is extremely difficult," Mark responds as he puts his basketball shoes in his bag.

Lance answers, "You think?"

"Yeah... How long have you all been married again?" Mark asks.

"It's going to be two years and six months in a couple weeks."

Mark laughs. "Man, you sound like you're talking about your 12 month, 16-day-old son!"

"Ha! You're funny. She won't let me forget, bro. She remembers the hour and all that! Very specific."

"True! They do have those impeccable memories. Except when it's not in their favor," Mark points out.

The two stand and start walking out of the gym. Lance replies, "Yup! You know, my lady wants to spend all of our money and she's not really cognizant of how much money is going in and out of the house. I can't stand living check to check, man. I'm trying to get ahead. That's why I joined the military." He shakes his head.

"Wendy likes to spend, but she has a job, so she spends my money first and then her own." Mark smirks. "She actually just started making a little more money than me, to be honest. Kind of demoralizing, because she has talked crap about it before." Mark doesn't understand why Wendy has to rub it in his face. They're supposed to be a team, not tear each other down. He pauses for a moment, thinking about their struggles.

"Did you hear me?" Lance interrupts Mark's daze.

"Hear what? Sorry, man."

Lance repeats himself, "I was saying that my wife doesn't have one of those. She does not even talk about getting a job. But wait—you said your lady makes more than you?" He turns his head and squints his face to see if he's understanding Mark correctly.

"Yeah... And it's not easy street with that setup. You think we all experience some of the same situations in marriage?" Mark wonders out loud.

"Of course we do. And then we don't, because my wife seems to not want a job, so she's not going to make more than me, I don't think."

Mark and Lance both laugh as they walk across the parking lot to their cars.

"Damn, you been on a roll today," Mark jokes.

"Indeed I have, haha. But don't get down, bro, things will get better. Just keep pushing, man." Lance pats Mark on the back.

"As always, my friend. I really appreciate it." The two shake hands as they hop in their cars. They are both going through challenging times in their marriage, but their friendship helps them know that they're not alone in their struggles.

Mark pulls out of the parking lot, honking a couple times as he passes his friend, thankful for their chat. He's in deep thought on the car ride home. Respect... Everybody wants to be respected. Mark wants to be treated like the *man of the house,* especially if he feels he's fulfilling his obligations as a man by being a decent husband and father. He feels is he is not getting the respect he deserves from his wife, and it's starting to boil inside of him.

***

Mark is leaving the base from the gym. As he's driving, a *dingggg* goes off on his phone, notifying him of a received text message. The message is from Wendy:

"Hey, can you keep an eye on Little Mark for a while? I want to go have a drink with some people from work later."

Mark hesitates before responding, thinking about how often Wendy has started hanging out after hours. Coming to a stop at a red light, he replies, **"That's fine. Who are you going with?"**

Wendy responds in all caps, **"PEOPLE FROM WORK... I just said that."**

He texts back through his verbal command on his iPhone since he's driving, **"So, everybody from work *question mark*. Your manager *dot dot dot*. And those females you don't get along with *question mark*."** He has to say it twice to get it to send the correct message, but he doesn't understand why his wife would want to hang out with people she doesn't even like.

Wendy sends, **"I'm going with April and them. Just a few people from work; you want me to name every single person?"**

Mark replies immediately. This time, he's looking down at his phone while driving and simultaneously looking back up at the road. **"I'm just asking a question, Wendy. It's not that serious."** Mark rolls his eyes.

Wendy responds, clearly frustrated, **"I didn't say it was. But I don't ask you every single person you go have drinks with, do**

I?! All I asked was if you can watch your own son for an evening."

Mark sends a message right back, "**I don't even go out like that. But you have been going out quite often. I don't interrogate…**" As Mark looks up, he has to slam on his brakes so he doesn't hit the car in front of him. His tires screech over the radio he had playing in the car. His heart beats rapidly as he feels the adrenaline from the close call. As the cars start to move, he pulls over into the gas station to finish his text. "**I don't even go out like that. But you have been going out quite often. I don't interrogate you every time, either.**" He starts to type another message on top of the one he just sent and then deletes what he's typing. He's upset with the way this conversation is going and it's really hard to find the right words to say.

He receives another message from Wendy saying, "**You go out enough. I'm going with some friends from work… simple as that.**"

Mark throws his phone into the passenger seat. He can't continue this discussion through text and is too frustrated to call. He grips the steering wheel tightly, feeling tense, and decides to just pause the conversation until he arrives home.

* * *

Wendy is making spaghetti after picking up Little Mark from daycare. She's at the stove making their plates while texting with Mark. She continues fixing her meal after sending the last message. Continually looking at her phone and waiting for a buzz, she walks a plate to Little Mark's highchair and places a green child-friendly fork in his food for him.

"I can't believe him," she says to herself, recalling the current topic of discussion. Knowing Mark will be home shortly, Wendy contemplates making his plate and ultimately decides against it. *He can make his own plate*, she thinks to herself as she seats herself and eats along with Little Mark.

An uncontrollable smile takes over Wendy's face as her son struggles to balance one strand of spaghetti on his fork. "You've eaten this before; you know what you're doing," she says to him.

He opens both of his tiny hands, spreading his arms as if he's waiting for a huge hug to come his way. He squints his eyes, opens his mouth wide, and slightly sticks out his little pink tongue because he knows what's coming next. As Wendy twirls some spaghetti on his fork and sticks it in his mouth, she says, "You're so spoiled."

Little Mark smiles as he chews, just knowing his mommy loves him.

Wendy's phone finally buzzes and she is ready to respond to her unreasonable husband. Instead, she sees a Facebook Messenger notification from her manager, Jody. She opens it and it reads, **"You're coming tonight, right?"**

She responds, **"Yes, we all need a little downtime from that work environment. I'm picking up April and we'll be there for**

sure." Wendy goes from considering cursing at Mark to smirking as she sends out a message to her associate.

Looking at the three dots indicating a reply is on its way, Wendy sees headlights in the living room window. She turns off her notifications for messenger and sets her phone down, knowing that Mark will walk in any second. As he enters, she stands from the table, wraps her plate with aluminum foil, and puts it in the refrigerator.

Mark shuts the door and removes his green combat boots. He heads into the kitchen in his camouflage ABUs and tan socks, kisses his son on the head, and says "Hey, buddy." He slips past Wendy, letting out a low, meaningless, "Hey."

This infuriates her and she says, "So, you're just going to walk right past me like that?"

Mark completely ignores her and drops his black book bag off in their room. Marks heads back to the kitchen, and Wendy passes him in the hall, her arms crossed. He proceeds to fix his plate and eat his food alongside Little Mark, while Wendy showers and gets ready to go hang out. While Mark is eating, he thinks about the current issue, not having much to say at all. He makes faces at Little Mark as they both eat. "Come on, man," He says after his son gets caught up in the playful moment and starts to pick the spaghetti up with his hands. Wiping his hands with a damp paper towel, he reminds his son, "Use your fork."

The two finish eating and Mark cleans up the table and Little

Mark's high chair. He then walks over to the living room when Little Mark has already migrated to play with his toys. Mark sits on the couch and changes the channel on the TV because he realizes the game is on.

After getting ready, Wendy walks over to the living room couch where Mark is sitting with Little Mark, watching the Brooklyn Nets play the Houston Rockets.

Standing in front of the TV in a tight black dress, she asks, "Can you transfer me some money?"

Raising his eyes to look past Wendy, Mark responds, "Why are you dressed like you're going on a date? And didn't you just get paid? Where's your money going?"

Wendy takes a step sideways to get back in his line of sight and says, "I did, but I also just paid 95% of our bills," ignoring his *date* statement.

"That isn't true at all and you know it. You keep more money in your pocket than I do! You just… never mind. Yes, I'll transfer you some money, okay?"

"I keep more because I make more… Thanks! You should do it for your wife without hesitating."

"Disrespectful as hell." Mark slightly raises his voice in frustration. "And I do all kinds of stuff for my wife."

"Like what? What exactly do you do for me?" she snaps.

"I send you flowers, I make extra efforts around the house, I walk around here on eggshells, I—"

Wendy cuts him off. "You do all of that for bragging rights, then? You just have to talk about it and put everything that you're doing out there, right? It doesn't matter if you're doing it just for recognition. And don't say you walk on eggshells for me."

"I'm not doing it for recognition!" Mark spouts back, feeling himself getting upset. Bringing his voice back down, "I do it to try to make you happy, but it obviously doesn't work. I'm just asking for you to be grateful. And those eggshells are real as they come. I can't talk to you about anything serious. Bills, money issues, nothing... All the while, you just worry about the next time you're going out."

"So, you do everything for Little Mark? Take him to daycare and all that? You're just a single parent, right? You pay all the bills like a man should? Do you do that for me, Mark?" she demands.

"That's not what I'm saying. And you just have to bring the money junk up every chance you get," he points out. "You literally just got a speeding ticket and who took care of things? Me! Right!? Even though you make soooo much more than me, I'm still taking care of all of *your* so-called financial responsibilities."

"You're supposed to do that! You're a man, aren't you? Stop complaining about what you're supposed to do as a man!" Wendy snaps.

70

"You should really stop watching that *Real Housewife* stuff because you sound just like them. But first off, lower your voice in front of our son. Second, I'm supposed to take care of everything you cause as an adult?" Mark replies.

"*Real Housewives*?! This isn't a time to play! And I didn't cause anything!" Wendy has told him multiple times the car in front of her was the one speeding. "Whatever! Okay! Are you transferring the money or what? I have to get ready." She turns to walk out of the house.

"Of course! Unfinished business, as usual!" Mark shouts disregarding his own request to calm down in front of their son.

Wendy turns back around and glares at Mark, "*You* can finish it! I'm going to go enjoy myself!"

"Yeah, that's new!" he yells back.

Wendy notices Little Mark has been lying quietly playing his LeapFrog tablet, like their argument doesn't even exist. She kisses him before leaving. "Yeah... Okay. Just take care of your son!" Wendy grabs her red handbag and storms out of the door.

"Sure! Anything for you!" Infuriated, Mark turns off the TV and throws the remote on the couch. He picks up his son and proceeds to giving him a bath so he can get ready for bed. While Little Mark plays in his bubble bath, Mark looks through his Facebook newsfeed. He notices a post Wendy put up. It shows her emotion as *feeling excited*. Her post reads, **"It's nice to get away from stress for a while. #Nightout #LetsDrink**

#StressRelief"

"You gotta be kidding me," he says to himself. Mark can't believe what he's reading. They've had discussions about expressing themselves on social media. This makes him feel like getting on the same page is next to impossible, because her putting their business on social media is welcoming even more issues and makes him feel she wants attention from somewhere else. He puts his phone down and focuses on taking care of his son.

TAKEAWAYS

When we address the RESPECT factor, we understand that it's something everybody desires. Most men get to the point of not wanting much from their wife, just respect. In my opinion, our generation differs from others with the things we see on TV, in movies, on YouTube, etc. We are living in an age where you come across examples of disrespect on a daily basis. It can be while you're scrolling down your newsfeed, or listening to a song on the radio. It's just another element that has been impacted by a changing world, which, in turn, can affect an individual's behavior.

Wendy and Mark obviously have a lack of respect for one another. What Mark sees in his wife is a woman who is never satisfied. He feels like it's a battle that just can't be won, especially with his wife making more money than him. She mentions something in coordination with that fact almost every time they get into a disagreement. This makes Mark feel somewhat inadequate, but he still feels he is doing his part as a man, regardless of their compared incomes. These struggles tend to be part of the reason he talks with his close friend Lance about situations. It's something about knowing that "you're not the only one going through this" that makes things not so bad. These conversations help both men.

It's ironic that Wendy was upset about Mark being gone

often with his sports, as now the roles have reversed with her hanging out with friends often in the evenings. She has been leaving the house more and more because it's an escape for her. She escapes the house, the responsibilities, and the inevitable tension between her and Mark.

Something that is becoming more of a subtle issue in their marriage is the fact that Wendy's work associate is now messaging her through social media. He has been sliding into her DM (Direct Message), and it's definitely a slippery slope.

At this stage in the marriage, couples have been together for about two to three years and are getting less patient with their partners. They are learning more about thought processes, habits, and other annoying attributes they didn't recognize before. I like to call this "the four-wall syndrome." When two people are in this phase of marriage and experiencing a lot of challenges, it feels like it's just them and those four walls, and they're closing in fast! Extreme patience can go a long way in this phase of a Millennial marriage.

7

COUNSELING

"Now, I know we said things,
Did things that we didn't mean
And we fall back into the same patterns, same routines..."

-Eminem
"Love The Way You Lie"

Mark is currently attending a small briefing held by his Commander. He doesn't really feel like being bothered by too many people today, so he sits as far back in the auditorium as he thinks he can get away with, without being called to move up and fill in seats. These briefings are typically fairly quick because the Squadron Commander gives out updates, a few awards, and is then on his way. One thing that Mark knows is always consistent is the fact that his Commander is almost always late. Knowing this, he has his iPhone out and is scrolling through social media. After speeding past the #TBT posts on Instagram, he closes the application and opens Facebook. Mark sees a post by Wendy that is a selfie of her blowing a kiss toward the phone. He doesn't "like" any of her pictures like this, but he does "like" it this time, hoping it helps a little with their less-than-ideal feelings toward each other.

Mark scrolls through her other likes and comments; he notices a name that seems familiar but he doesn't know how. *Jody Mays.* On top of liking Wendy's picture, Jody comments, saying, **"Where did this kiss land?"** There was a blushing emoji face at the end of the comment. Mark immediately gets a little hot inside and can feel his heart speed up a few beats. He looks through some of Wendy's other pictures and sees the same person giving her attention pretty regularly. After multiple comments and likes, Mark is infuriated because after looking through this Jody character's page, he also sees some reciprocation from Wendy on Jody's posts. Hearing seats bounce back to their original position, Mark puts his phone away and stands at attention with the rest of his squadron. Watching his Commander walk across the stage, all he can think about is what he just witnessed.

After his Commander's Call concludes, Mark jumps back on his phone to confront Wendy. He texts her, **"Who is Jody?"**

***

Wendy is reviewing a prescription with a patient when her phone beeps with a text message. She puts her hand in her pocket and slides her ringer to vibrate. "Sorry about that," she says to the patient.

Her patient, a sweet middle-aged lady, responds, "Don't be sorry sweetie, that's just fate calling telling you to hurry up with my medicine." The lady smiles playfully at Wendy, sensing her need for a little humor. Wendy is receptive to the light joke and smiles responding, "You're going to be able to get it very soon, Ms. Mays."

Once Wendy is done with her patient, she looks at her phone and sees Mark's text. She hesitates on answering, not opening the message completely to leave it unread. Wendy holds off because doesn't really know what to say and feels trouble looming. On one hand, she doesn't see anything wrong, but on the other, she remembers all the communication she and Jody have had on social media. That's her main concern with the question. She knows there's been a lot of interaction between them online and also knows that Mark is likely referring to that because he doesn't know her supervisor at all. She's never talked about him in any of their conversations. She sits at her desk and decides to go ahead and respond. **"Jody is my supervisor. Why?"**

Mark: **"Oh really? So, it's your supervisor liking and**

commenting on all of your pictures?"

Wendy: "A lot of people like and comment on my posts. I have a lot of friends."

Mark: "But your supervisor, though? Seriously? And I see you return the favor quite a bit…"

Wendy: "I don't say anything with your liking and commenting on people's posts."

Mark: "Well, it's not many females I'm liking and commenting on, and they definitely aren't my supervisor!"

Wendy: "It's really not a big deal. "

Mark: "WTH do you mean, it's not a big deal!? You're exchanging likes and comments with a man that you work with!"

Wendy: "He's my supervisor!!! That's it!!"

Mark reads Wendy's last message and is completely infuriated. Trying to keep his cool at work, he holds his phone's power button and swipes right on the screen to turn it off. He can't even endure another ridiculous text message right now. His supervisor walks in and asks if he's done with his break because he needs him to look after the other Airman while they're doing their work. Mark replies saying "I'll be right out," and proceeds to lock his computer to get out on the floor with his co-workers.

***

A few weeks pass and things haven't settled well with Mark. The couple have had a bad falling out that didn't seem like it was recoverable. Mark and Wendy decide to start attending formal counseling. Wendy, however, has already been participating in informal counseling with her mother, who is trying to reassure her that things will be ok. Her mother is doing a good job of reassuring her daughter, but now they need a professional's help to guide them through this difficult time in their marriage.

Wendy calls her mom from work like she usually does. But this time, the conversation is more serious.

"You're going to counseling now?" Wendy's mom asks.

Wendy sighs, "Unfortunately, yes... I guess we're trying to save what's left of this marriage."

"Baby, don't talk like that. Everything is going to be fine. I'm sure you and Mark will work through this. Marriage is a constant compromise and it's not easy by any means. It's not supposed to be, either. The journey is what makes it all worth it," she assures her daughter. "I've never heard you talk like this before." Wendy starts to perk up, adjusting her phone to make sure she's hearing everything her mother says.

"Well, I haven't had to, but I do know the struggles of marriage all too well."

"I don't feel like we're going to have another baby together. I think that hurts me most," Wendy states.

"Maybe that's not the best thing to focus on right now," her mother says for the first time. "You two need to focus on each other."

"The baby *will* be us focusing on each other. Little Mark is growing so fast and I just feel like it's being delayed so much that it's not going to happen. Now we're doing counseling and all of this extra stuff. I'm so done." Wendy shakes her head. She's not sure if she has what it takes to stick this out any further.

"Wendy, you're fine, okay? Focus on you and your husband's relationship and everything else will fall into place."

"Okay, Mom. I love you. I'm about to leave work."

"Okay. Love you too, Wendy."

Wendy hangs up the phone and has started packing up her stuff to leave for the day when her cute supervisor slips over.

"Hey, Sunshine, or should I say, Sunset, since we're leaving?"

😃

"Oh, hey." Wendy doesn't make eye contact. She keeps packing her things.

"Are you good? I haven't seen you out in a few weeks. You know we got drinks last Friday, right? I sent you a text about it." He questions her with a worried look on his face.

"Yeah, I saw that. I've just been dealing with some things at home. And honestly, my husband hasn't been too fond of our conversing with each other."

Mark thinks Wendy's relationship with her supervisor at work is way too friendly. Even though she says it's harmless, he's trying to force her to end it. She questions his trust for her, but he says it's not that he doesn't trust her, he just doesn't trust other men.

"Really? Not fond of us having friendly conversations? Why is that?" Jody asks.

"He doesn't feel like it's appropriate for us to talk like that. And plus, you've been liking my pictures on social media, Mr. Creeper." Wendy pushes out a smile and then laughs out loud at her own joke. She has been so down lately, she can't help but to let that laugh take over.

"Creeper? Lol, I'm sorry, I don't mean to get you into trouble. I don't know what there is to worry about, anyway. I mean, first off, you'd never give me the time of day, and second, you're Miss Goody-Two-Shoes," he teases.

"Miss Goody-Two-Shoes? What in the world are you talking about?" Wendy asks with a puzzled look on her face.

"Lol, you know what I'm saying. I don't mean it like that; you just seem so well put together. Work, family; everything just seems like it's right under your control, you know?"

"Well, since you put it like that," Wendy says, lifting her head with a sense of confidence.

:)

"Lol! But hey, I don't mean to be disruptive to your marriage. My bad," her supervisor says. "I don't like getting things stirred up. I just want to take care of these patients and make sure you all are being nice to them." He winks regarding the patient comment.

"Oh, stop, we're all nice to the patients. Except Tammy. She's not that nice to them when they come in late." Wendy says.

They both have a laugh about that because the whole clinic knows Tammy doesn't like it when patients come in late. "And don't worry, you're not causing any more harm in my marriage than what's already there." Wendy rolls her eyes.

"Ooookkkkkkay. Well, in that case, how about a quick drink after work?" her supervisor jokes and then picks right back up. "Kidding. I know you have things to take care of."

:D

"Yeah, I do, I'm sorry. Maybe some other time; I might be able to come with you guys again one of these lucky weekends."

"Sounds like a plan to me. If you ever need anything, I'm there for you. Have a great night, Wendy!" Jody says, as he turns to get his things from his office.

"Thanks," she responds. "You too." Wendy does notice the flirting that her supervisor does with her, and can see how it can be off-putting to her husband, but she still doesn't see the harm in being friends with him. For a moment, she thinks about how it would make her feel.

She walks under the orange exit sign as on her way out of the clinic and says bye to Delores, the cleaning lady. She doesn't think she'd react the same way as Mark if the roles were reversed.

***

Mark and Wendy get home almost at the same time. They decide to take Little Mark to the neighborhood park for a few minutes. It's Mark's idea and Wendy reluctantly agrees, even though she's not up to it. Upon arriving at the park, Little Mark takes off and starts climbing the brown playground stairs to go down the slide.

Wendy sits down on the park bench. She's surprised to see that it's such a nice evening outside and they're the only ones at the park. She sees Mark greet Little Mark at the end of the slide and then start chasing his son around in the brown mulch.

After running around for a few minutes, Mark sits down by Wendy. "We should try to get him signed up for some sports or something. He's getting big super-fast," suggests Mark.

"Then do it," Wendy flatly replies.

"What sport do you think we should look into?"

"I don't know. Whatever you're thinking, I guess." She shrugs as if she doesn't care about this at all. She can't help but to think

83

about all of the problems they're having and wondering when Mark will change his ways.

Puzzled at her reaction, Mark asks, "So, you don't want to take part in this? It could be exciting."

"You brought it up. You figure it out," Wendy states blandly.

"What's your problem? Can we at least come together to do something for our child?" Mark asks.

"So, you can't do something yourself for once?"

"I don't even understand why *we* can't just discuss this like adults. *We* obviously need to figure out a way to communicate. We can't even have a conversation that pertains to our kid."

The counselor has advised them to refrain from using words like *"you"* because of the offense it can cause the receiver of the message.

Wendy yells back, "Here you go again with the 'WE' crap! So, a man tells you that we should stop saying 'You' and 'I' when addressing things, and you have to say something about it every chance you get?"

"Isn't that what counseling is? Aren't we supposed to be putting forth the effort to fix this situation?"

"So, our marriage is a *situation*?" Her face hardens with anger.

"What the hell, Wendy? Can we act our age for a few minutes? I'm not doing anything but asking about getting our son into sports, and now look where we are! Where we always are!" He throws his arms up in the air.

"I'm not anywhere. You're the one trying to argue. Not me."

"So, I'm going back and forth with myself now? Why does it feel like I'm the only one fighting for us!?"

"Why does it feel like you can't understand what I need from you?" she retorts.

"What is it that you need from me then?" he demands.

Wendy screams, " I want you to be a man!"

"I'm not?! I take care of my family, work my ass off, and I'm faithful, which is more than I can say for you!"

"I told you it was and is nothing!" she yells.

"So, confiding in another man is nothing!? How would you like it if I found another woman to talk to?"

"You are either going to forgive me or you're not!" Wendy feels like Mark will never let this go.

"This doesn't even have anything to do with that. All I'm asking you to do is talk to me with some respect! Talk to me, period! We're wasting all this time in counseling and you still can't get it!"

They both sort of forget that they're outside at the neighborhood park and out in the open with their argument. This is how serious it has gotten, because they typically dislike their personal business being exposed.

"If it's wasted time, why are we still going?" Wendy snarls.

She stands up and storms off away from the park. She doesn't even go toward home while walking off.

***

"You tell me…" Mark mutters to himself, watching his wife walk away in anger.

Everything they're going through and all of the effort he's been putting forth flashed right before his eyes. Frustration has overwhelmed him because he doesn't feel that his effort to make things work is matched by hers, and now he has to deal with the fact that she's been communicating with another man. He's starting to see no end to the continued difficulties.

As he turns around to face forward on the park bench, he sees Little Mark running in the mulch like somebody is chasing him. Uncontrollably smiling, Mark feels grateful that his son seems to not notice the difficulties his parents are experiencing.

TAKEAWAYS

In the counseling phase, there is some formal and informal counseling taking place. Counseling is something that people have different perspectives about; when it comes to formal counseling, you either think it's beneficial and are willing to go through the process and work at it, or you think counseling is a waste of time and won't fix anything. There's hardly ever any in-between with this subject. Informal counseling comes into play with people who lend an ear for couples. If utilized effectively, formal counseling, informal counseling, or consoling conversations with people you're close to can help you look at circumstances in a different light. At this point, anything positive that anyone has to say is absolutely encouraging.

Mark and Wendy are attending formal counseling. Wendy is also informally counseling with her mother, who is trying to reassure her that things will be okay. She gives great advice when Wendy brings up another baby. She tells her to focus on their relationship and everything else will fall into place. This advice can go a long way if implemented. Millennials sometimes focus on many different aspects of a situation, rather than the ultimate issue that can help mend the other factoring issues.

Mark has found out about Wendy's communications with Mr. Friendly. Even though she says it's harmless, he's feeling betrayed by the discovery. Frustration has overwhelmed him because he doesn't feel that his effort to make things work is matched by hers, and now he has to get over the fact that she has been talking to another man.

Living in the Millennial era, communicating with people has been expanded to much more than just letters or cordless phones. It takes two seconds to "like" a picture on Facebook, acknowledging the fact that you're aware of an appealing picture that somebody posted. All it takes is one picture for that person to start "liking" your pictures in return. This can sometimes send mixed signals.

When getting married, or even when considering marriage, standpoints on social media should be discussed. Social media has been the culprit in many struggling and failed relationships. If they find a middle ground for the subject early on, couples can avoid any social media mishaps or surprises.

I offer the same recommendation for pre-marital counseling. Marriage counseling before tying the knot can bring forth any potential disagreements that can be properly addressed before a couple is out on their own, knee-deep into someone else's life.

8

THE EYE OF THE STORM

"Girl, what's your problem
Cause I know it's hard sometimes,
Baby, just give it some time
Oh, honey, now, girl, we can solve them
If you just give me some time I can open up your mind..."

-Childish Gambino
"Sober"

Mark and Wendy's counseling sessions seem to turn out well. Over a year has passed, and life is moving very quickly. They're getting along just as well as they ever have. So well that they have some news they've been waiting to share—they're on their way to having another child, and also on their way to another duty station. Mark and Wendy have found a nice balance in their lives and are eager to begin a new chapter, including today when they're out with Little Mark at the zoo.

Walking through the Philadelphia Zoo, Wendy sees a brown adult monkey playing with a smaller monkey that looks to be the child. She places her hand on her stomach, smiling. She says to Mark, "Baby, I'm so happy! We're going to have a little girl! This is so exciting!" Wendy's grin spreads across her entire face. This moment seems like it has taken forever to come.

"It really is. I wonder who she's going to look like, because you know Little Mark looks just like Big Mark, right?" he boasts.

"Oh, please. He has your chin and I'm sure that's about it."

"No way. Look at this—hey, Little Mark, come here." He waves his son over. It takes a couple of attempts to get his four-year-old child to run over because his eyes are locked in on the animals he's seeing.

Finally coming over, Little Mark says, "Hey, Daddy," while simultaneously grabbing his father's hand.

"Who do you think you look like—me or Mommy?"

Little Mark thinks really hard while looking back and forth between his parents' faces. "Ummmm, Mommy??"

Wendy laughs, "Ah ha ha ha ha! Told you!"

"No, big head, you look like me. Lol." Mark rubs his hand on his son's head, messing up his hair.

"Okay, I look like Daddy," Little Mark says excitedly. The good energy from the moment is having a positive effect on the entire family. The vibes feel much better than when they were in the counseling phase.

"Whatever! He already answered; he knows who he looks like," Wendy says.

Little Mark runs off to the gorilla viewing area. "That's far enough," Wendy tells him.

It feels good for the family to be happy again and in a positive state of mind. Mark looks lovingly into Wendy's eyes. "Okay, if you have him, she's definitely going to be mine."

"If you say so. Have you heard any more about us moving to a new base?"

"No, not really. I mean, we have seven months left here and we're going to Scott in Illinois. That's about it until it's time to out-process. I guess we're getting a little closer to home," he jokes. Going from New Jersey to Missouri is not the ideal move when wanting to get closer to home, but they're both happy nonetheless.

"When is that? When do we out-process?" Wendy asks.

"Probably about a couple months or so," Mark says. "They still have me working like a bloodhound."

"Well, at least you're working like a bloodhound there, because you're sure not doing it at the house," Wendy replies.

"That's the cost of doing business, baby," Mark says.

The couple seems to have found their spark again, joking about things that usually cause an argument.

"Yeah, yeah. We're lucky my job transfers there, because I don't think your job alone could sustain our lifestyle," Wendy laughs.

"Ha….Ha… How about I joke on you?" he teases.

"Don't go there." Wendy laughs while grabbing Little Mark's hand.

"Okay, I'll let you keep taking those shots, it's fine. I know you're fragile, so I won't say anything about those fingers you call toes, lol."

"Now we're getting personal because my feet are on point!" she answers, putting her hands on her hips.

"You're right. Hey, we have some good things going. I think by this time next year, we are going to be set up pretty nicely." Mark smiles proudly.

"We will be. We just have to keep doing what we're doing," she replies. "Our family will be a plus one, and we'll be settling in to our new life!"

"Yeah, that's true. I see you're using 'we,' huh? Lol!" Mark teases. He teases her about things from counseling because she was reluctant to buying into the sessions initially, thinking counseling was not going to help their situation.

"Yup, I guess so. I might just be tired of hearing you say it, so I'm using it subconsciously." Wendy laughs and pokes him.

"Subconsciously. That's a good way to put it. So, are we going to go to dinner after this or what?" he asks.

"If you're paying."

"I wouldn't expect anything less. Save all your money while we spend all of mine. Living the dream."

😉

"At least you know it! Lol." Wendy chuckles.

They continue their tour through the zoo and head out to dinner at a nice restaurant. The evening goes by smoothly and the two relax and enjoy a family movie together later that evening. Everything is back on track...

TAKEAWAYS

Mark and Wendy have experienced very challenging times in their relationship, but things seem to be finally falling into place. Sometimes this phase can be even better than newlyweds or the Glory Days because while going through the difficult stages, it just seems like it'll never get better. This phase can bring a sense of satisfaction and also complacency.

Complacency can be a sore thumb to a marriage. It's better to be content than to be complacent. Being content can make happiness contagious in marriage. Being complacent can do just the opposite. When a couple is content, they're grateful for what they have and how far they've come. They recognize the struggles and are happy with what they've created while overcoming those struggles.

Complacency brings along old habits, ones that may not be the best to remember. Steadily working for the marriage is not something you get complacent about; it's a never-ending effort. Luckily, most military marriages get addicted to the feeling of this phase and find the formula to making it last.

9

THIS AGAIN!?

"I'm good, I'm good, I'm great
Know it's been a while, now I'm mixing up the drank
I just need a girl who gon' really understand
I just need a girl who gon' really understand..."

-The Weekend
"Party Monster"

Over a year has passed since Wendy and Mark moved and settled into their new base. Their daughter is a little over a year old and has just started daycare. She's growing right before her parents' eyes. Mark and Wendy have also settled into new friendships, which have brought about some different but familiar choices. Wendy has a group of girlfriends that she hangs with and they aren't the best of influences.

Mark has also found a few friends that he plays sports and video games with pretty often. Both have started to get irritated by one another and have been slipping back into old behaviors.

Walking into their bedroom that is blacked out with curtains at 2:00 p.m., Mark sees his wife moving around underneath the covers. "Good morning or afternoon! You're finally awake, huh?" Mark sings.

Still rolling around in the bed, Wendy replies, "Why are you so loud?" She has a headache because she's been out all night.

"Why is this your second time going out in two weeks?"

"Isn't it obvious? Because I wanted to, right?!" Wendy yells.

"When are you going to learn, Wendy? That stuff should be a thing of the past. You're still acting like you're twenty-one."

"Well, I'm an adult and can go out if I choose to!" Wendy rolls her eyes and puts the pillow over her head.

"Age doesn't determine whether you're an adult," he says. "You're proving that. You are deliberately doing things I don't want you to do!"

"It's not about what you want. You don't control me," she says from underneath the pillow.

"I'm not trying to, but you're married and you can't compromise with your husband!" Mark yells back.

"There's no compromise. I want to go enjoy myself and you don't want me to, so I'm going to do what makes me happy and enjoy life."

"Do you listen to yourself when you talk? Four in the morning and that's what makes you happy!? You are completely selfish and you can't even see it. Me and the kids are at the house by ourselves pretty much every weekend, and that's life to you?" he shouts.

"Don't bring the kids into this—I break my back for them!"

"Where? At your job? Breaking your back at home is kind of hard to believe, seeing that they eat fast food every day!" Mark slings the curtain open to get some sunlight into the room.

"Oh my God!" Wendy says in frustration. "I take care of my kids, okay? So, you can quit bringing them into this! And you can cook something too, right!?"

"I literally just cooked two nights ago, but you wouldn't remember because Thursday night is ladies' night..."

"What, some dry chicken?!" Wendy yells. That's what you call cooking? You might as well not do it at all!" Wendy finally rises out of the bed.

"Ungrateful. Unappreciative. Selfish. So many words to describe you!"

"And I can describe you with all kind of negative words, too, with your nagging! If you're going to complain about something, you need to be ready to do it yourself!" she snaps.

"And I DO!!! WHAT'S SO HARD TO UNDERSTAND ABOUT THIS?! YOU WORK, DRINK, PARTY, COMPLAIN ABOUT ME, AND THAT'S IT!! I'M TIRED OF THIS!" Mark screams in a rage.

Wendy puts her pounding head in her hands. "Here you go with this damn yelling! Stop yelling at me like that, OKAY!"

"We've been yelling this whole time and now it's a problem because I get a little louder!? I can't deal with this!!" Mark says as he bends over the dresser, hanging his head.

"You don't have to! I'm not holding you back!"

"I'm glad you think it's you! You sit there pretending we don't have two kids! If it wasn't for them..."

Wendy cuts him off, "If it wasn't for them, what? You'd be gone? Huh!?"

"What you think?"

Wendy stands and screams in Mark's face, "Then GO! GO! GET OUT! NOW!"

"Wendy, get out of my FACE! RIGHT NOW!" Mark threatens.

Wendy retorts, "NO, *YOU* LEAVE!"

The bedroom door swings open and their son is standing in the doorway with his pajamas on. "Stop it, guys!" Little Mark says sadly.

"Come on, Mark, go to your room... you have to go to your room, buddy." Mark tries to convince his son to leave, as to not fight in front of him.

Little Mark cries, "No, Daddy. You guys are fighting... I don't want you to fight!"

It breaks Mark's heart to hear this.

"Go to your room, Mark. Mommy and Daddy are talking,"

Mark tries again.

"No, you're not," sobs little Mark.

Wendy shrieks, "Go to your room, Mark!"

"Don't raise your voice at him! He hasn't done anything! The kid is right!" Mark hollers back.

"You're listening to a child now?" Wendy says snarkily.

"He's not right?!" demands Mark. "Look at the example we're setting for him! This is okay with you!?"

"Just GET OUT!" Wendy shoves toward Mark to leave the room, too.

"CHILL OUT LIKE THAT AROUND HIM!" Mark shouts back.

"Daddy, nooo!" the child wails.

"Mark, go to YOUR ROOM!" Now he's yelling at his son, too, and not happy with himself. Little Mark runs crying down the hallway.

This incident takes Mark's heart and he is more hurt than he has ever been. "DAMN! "Now I'm yelling at him! We're just no good for them…"

☹

"Like I said, that's fine with me. Just get out of my house!" Wendy exclaims.

"This isn't your house… But that's just one more thing you don't understand. I'm out, Wendy…" Mark marches off down the hallway as well.

"BYE!" Wendy slams the door behind him.

***

Mark drives to the store to grab a drink.

"AAAHHHHHHH! What am I supposed to do?" he cries out loud to himself. "Please tell me what I'm supposed to do! I can't deal with this. I keep trying to do the right thing and it all just falls apart! God, I don't want to do this! I can't! Please tell me what to do!"

Mark pounds on the steering wheel. "I have to do it! It'll never get better! AAAHHHHHHH! What the F***! I have to leave! This isn't going to work for the kids! I gotta do better for them!" Mark is in such a bad spot, he can't even call anybody for support. He can only let his anger and emotion out in a rage in his car. He's praying in pain and anger all at once.

He holds a picture up of the kids and the tears start to stream down his face. "They need me, though. Why does this have to be so hard? Just... damn..." he sobs.

TAKEAWAYS

Mark and Wendy both realize how far apart they are drifting and each urges the other to make changes. They understand that they may be part of the problems they are experiencing, but their egos get in the way of real progression. This creates a toxic environment and brings forth a world of unhappiness that simply isn't the best situation when children are involved.

This phase is one of the toughest phases to deal with because there were high hopes for the future in the previous phase. Now, there is only confusion, frustration, and a lot of anger. From here, things only get harder with the hopes of change. One way or the other.

Mark and Wendy are having issues with the lifestyle they've chosen. She has issues with the way he spends his time, but he feels it's less impactful than the choices she makes. He plays video games daily and sports still play a large role in his life.

Sometimes, when getting married at a young age, an individual realizes how much of their adult life has been spent trying to play the marriage role instead of enjoying the party life all of their friends are currently living. It's enticing when you see your peers having fun and seemingly enjoying life by frequently partying and going out. A long week at work can make this choice an easy one to make. If married with children, a counterpart can perceive this as a lack of appropriate prioritization. Choosing to be married and having kids can ultimately lead to necessary sacrifices in certain areas of life. Not everybody sees it this way and it can be a significant obstacle in a marriage.

Mark doesn't really agree with the way Wendy is living, and he wants her to put her family first and to start acting like a married mother. The way he sees it, a married mother should not be partying every weekend every chance she gets. She, on the other hand, wants Mark to grow up from the video games and give more attention to the family. Both parties realize this isn't the best scenario for their children, and when tempers are at their peak, mistakes are made.

This leads to Mark a dark place of drinking and simultaneously looking at life with the question of, "What am I supposed to do?"

10

DECISIONS, DECISIONS

"I don't love her, I tried to tell myself
But you can see it in my eyes
So don't deny, I can't fool no one else
The truth is in the tears I cry..."

-New Edition
"If It Isn't Love"

Mark and Wendy have hit a breaking point in their marriage. This is a "fight or flight" situation. Either fight for your family to try to keep them together, or get out and hope that you're making the right choice. Wendy seems to have already given up on their chances of making it. Wendy calls her mom for support, "Mom, I really don't want to talk about it anymore. I'm just tired of dealing with it."

"Wendy, you can't be too tired of dealing with anything in this type of situation. You two are married. And you have children together; you need to take this seriously."

"I *am* taking it seriously," Wendy insists, "I just can't keep going through the same things over and over."

"What do you think the problem is, Wendy?" her mom asks.

"I think the problem is that Mark doesn't respect me enough to see that I'm a grown woman and I can make my own decisions."

"What do you mean? Is he controlling or something?"

Wendy retorts, "Yes! Anything I do, he just can't accept it. He complains nonstop about me going out with my friends and just having fun in general. It's like he wants me to stay in the house and be miserable."

"Do you go out a lot? Hanging with your friends and all?" her mother pries.

"That's not the point. I go when I get good and ready to because that's my decision."

"Well, if he doesn't like you doing certain things, you should at least consider or listen to where he's coming from," her mother advises.

"I *do* listen, and I *do* know where he's coming from." Wendy replies.

"How would you feel if it were him hanging out?"

"It's not that he doesn't hang out sometimes; I think he's just unhappy with himself, so he's wanting me to be unhappy."

"I remember when I used to love going to hang out with my friends," her mother says. "You know your dad wouldn't mind, but when I started going more often, that's when we had our own issues. He used to say 'Is that more important than your family?' Lol."

"What? I didn't know you used to go out." Wendy starts to realize she may be more like her mother than she thought.

"That's because you were just a child. I eventually stopped when I saw it was causing problems for my family. You were so young, you needed me there."

"Dad sounds just like Mark! That's crazy, Mom!" Wendy exclaims.

"Yup. I guess when you get married at a young age, things get sort of… confusing. You're so young, and yet you have responsibilities of somebody older than you."

"You know, I didn't want to talk about this anymore, but you know how to pull things out of me, don't you?" Wendy jokes.

"That's what I do."

***

Mark has taken on new habits to express how he feels and reflects on everything going on in his relationship. Writing in his journal has been one of a few changes he's made in his personal life to try to cope with his circumstances. Writing is very therapeutic and by journaling, he's come to a realization that he can't force Wendy to make any changes to her personality or decision-making. He now understands that the best way to change his conditions is to change himself.

Mark's journal entry:

Yesterday, Little Mark asked me not to leave our home. It came out of nowhere, and I asked him what he was talking about. He just repeated himself and said, "Daddy, just don't leave our home."

Man, it cut me to the core. We weren't even doing anything and he could just sense the pain. It killed me. I'm going to have to dig deep for this. I want to keep my family together; that's the best thing for the kids. I understand that I can be divorced and still be a great father for them, but the last thing I want to do is have them going from household to household. They'll understand everything when the time is right, but if I can't tell them that I did everything I possibly could to make things work, I'll feel like I'm failing them.

I just really want her to understand that I want the best for all of us. Not just me, not just the kids, but all of us. It doesn't matter if we're together or not; I still want her to be happy. If she's happy, she'll be able to keep them happy. And that's ultimately what I want. A toxic environment together is way more detrimental to their future than two households that are suitable.

I'm realizing that I can't just make her change. Change has to come from within, something you have to want to do for yourself. I have to change my approach with her, and change my tactics with this whole situation. The best way to change somebody else is to change yourself. I'm ready for change, and I know it has to start with me... wish me luck.

-Mark

***

"Hey Wendy, can we talk..."

"That's all we ever do," she mutters.

"Yeah, that and argue, but we need to talk about us, where we're headed in our relationship. The type of example we're setting for our kids. We can't keep living like this," Marks says.

Wendy sighs, "I know."

"How can we make this work? Or do you think we *can* make this work?" Mark sincerely wants to know.

"What do you think?"

"I just asked you," he points out.

"But I want you to tell me if you think we can make it work." Wendy says again.

"Honestly, it depends on whether we can actually listen to each other's needs and think about what we can do to satisfy each other. I want us to provide the best possible life for our children. It starts with what they see at home," Mark responds.

"So, you don't think we can make it?"

"That's not what I said... not at all. I'm just saying that if we're able to work on ourselves, we'll be fine. And if not, we have a serious future ahead of us."

"So, what are you saying? That we're going to divorce if we can't make things work?" Wendy starts to look sad.

"No, Wendy; can we please be sensible about this for a moment?" Mark pleads. "This is serious stuff."

"I *am* being serious!" Wendy yells, "But you're talking about changes, and you have yet to recognize the changes you need to make!"

Mark lets out a deep breath. "I don't want to argue about this; we can't argue about this."

"Then don't start this stuff because I don't feel like it!" Wendy starts to walk off.

Mark goes after her, turns her around, and kisses her. Wendy starts sobbing. "I'm soooo sorry... I know I haven't been putting you all first. I'm so selfish!"

"No, listen; it's both of us. What we've created isn't on you or me, it's both of us, Wendy. I really want things to change. It has to start now. We have to start now," Mark begs.

Little Mark walks in. "Mommy, why are you crying? Are you guys fighting again?"

"No baby, come here." Wendy opens her arms and embraces her son.

"We're okay, son; everything is going to be fine." Mark starts

MILLENNIAL MARRIAGES - "A MILITARY RELATIONSHIP"

sobbing uncontrollably, simultaneously turning his head away from his son, not wanting him to see. He forces words out of his mouth saying, "I love you all so much…"

Their daughter Miley quietly enters the room looking like a curious toddler. She walks up as the family is hugging to get some attention herself. Mark reaches over to pick her up as his son speaks up.

"I love you Daddy. I love you, too, Mommy. I love you, too, Miley, " Little Mark says.

With tears falling from her face, Wendy answers her son, "I love you, sweetie." They all hug one another, knowing that they will get through this together.

TAKEAWAYS

In this "fight or flight" situation, Wendy seems to have already given up on their chances of making it. She confides in her mom and it sounds like she feels her marriage with Mark is a lost cause. Mark feels the same way; however, he has taken on new habits to express how he feels and reflect on everything. Writing in his journal has been one of a few changes he has made in his personal life to try to cope with his circumstances. Based on Mark's journal entry, he has come to a realization that he can't force Wendy to make any changes to her personality or decision-making. He now understands that the best way to change his conditions is to change himself. This is a concept many Millennials could benefit from, because when they want things to be different between them and their partners, they do their best to tell them exactly what they want and need in order to be satisfied with their relationship. On the other hand, "What do you need from me?" could be an impactful approach rather than constantly expressing "What I need from you." Being selfless and taking a serious look in the mirror can be the spark of a new and extremely rewarding chapter in a Millennial marriage. To take advantage of this concept and approach, a person has to dig deep, fighting the good fight with weapons they've never used.

CLOSING STATEMENTS

Marriage has often been a challenging commitment throughout the years, but Millennials are dealing with more variables than any other generation has ever experienced. From the internet and social media to reality TV shows and movies, there are influences that Millennials must adapt to that the marriages before them never knew. Adding these variables to a Military Relationship makes the challenge that much more complicated. Starting off with the military stigma of getting married to be together applies pressure from the start. A young newly married couple can be heavily tested with certain military obligations, like deployments, demand on time, etc. There are real sacrifices being made by military couples and it's not always easy to persevere through the hardships, especially when they're away from family and trying to make it on their own.

Getting married at a young age can bring two people together who do not have a clear vision for their future, but as time passes and visions develop, it's a real test to keep trying to stay on the same page. Couples do not remain stagnant in these circumstances. They either grow together or they grow apart. When the challenges become overwhelming, married individuals can feel like they are alone and the only ones experiencing what they are going through. This is far from the truth. By seeking positive support, you can strengthen the chances of your marriage's survival. By having empathy, practicing effective communication, and by being selfless, we can renew the meaning of marriage. As Millennials, we do encounter great obstacles in marriage, but we also have the power to change the new culture of this sacred commitment.

–Millennial Marriages–

"A Military Relationship"

ABOUT THE AUTHOR

Jarron Webster is Kentucky native who left home in 2008 to spend eight years in the military. He is now an Air Force veteran residing in the Tampa, FL area. He is an inspirational speaker who aims to encourage and motivate people across the nation. Also, he currently works in real estate and takes pride in helping families make one of the biggest investment decisions of their lives. He has established a signature brand for himself and is known as The "Tampa Bow Tie Guy." Mr. Webster is a master's degree graduate in business administration, accomplished through Argosy University in Tampa. Mr. Webster lives to provide a great life for his two sons and make a positive and significant impact on as many other lives as possible. His favorite quote is by the great Zig Ziglar, "You will get all you want in life, if you help enough other people get what they want."

Mr. Webster can be contacted for book signings and other events here:

TampaBowTieGuy@gmail.com

You can also contact him via Facebook or Instagram:
-Tampa Bow Tie Guy

www.ingramcontent.com/pod-product-compliance
Lightning Source LLC
Chambersburg PA
CBHW071229090426
42736CB00014B/3021